Classic American Sedans of the 1950s

The Four-Doors

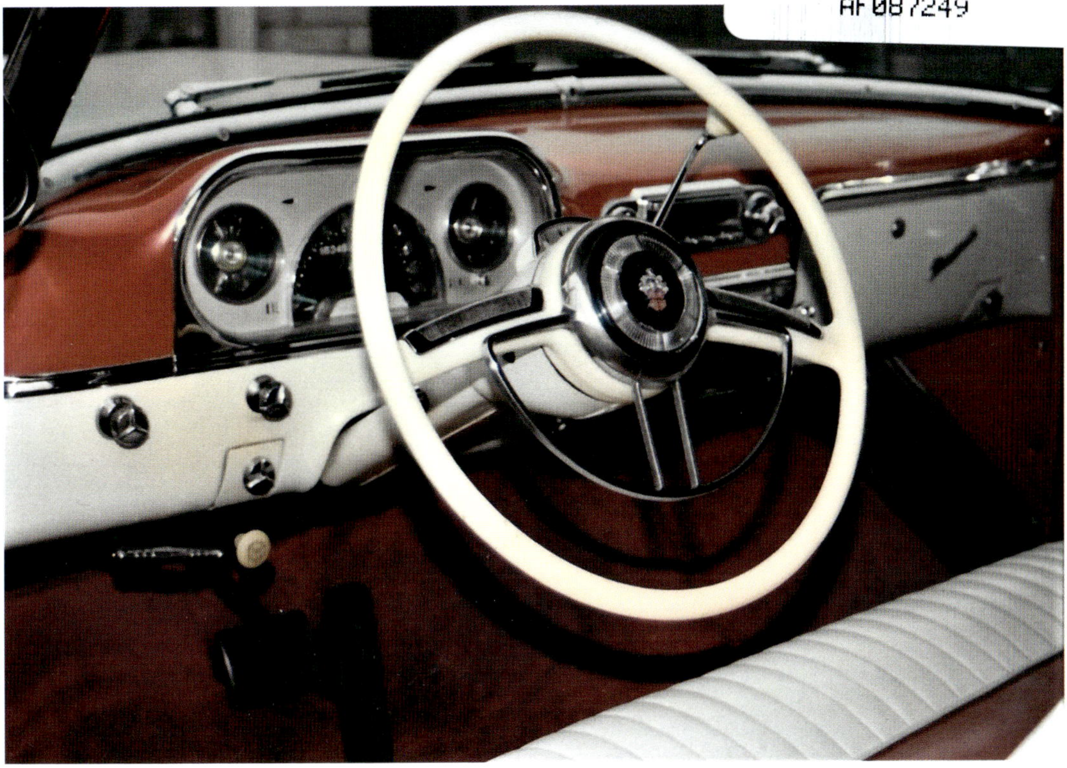

NORM MORT

KEY Books

Front cover image: Dripping with chrome typical of American cars of the fifties, this 1950 Studebaker was adorned with jet-age styling cues, from the nacelle-like opening on its nose to the aircraft canopy-styled rear window and fuselage-shaped body.

Title page image: The dashboard of 1950s American sedans had moved on from the Art Deco designs of the 1930s to draw inspiration from the layout and controls of aircraft. Although very limited in gauges, the chrome, levers, knobs, grilles and painted metal provided drivers with stylish functionality and flamboyant design.

Contents page image: By 1953, all American models other than pickup trucks were clothed in bodies of a more aerodynamic envelope; the accentuated rear fenders slowly faded away, as can be seen on this 1953 Chevrolet. By 1955, slab sides heralded a general move to smoother, cleaner lines. Visors on the front windshield and fender skirts would also begin to disappear by the end of the decade, as would the surfeit of chrome.

Back cover image: Hood ornaments on cars were a source of instant identity for some automakers from the earliest years of the 20th century. Best known were the Rolls-Royce Flying Lady, the three-pointed star of Mercedes-Benz and Pierce-Arrow's kneeling archer, while there was also the Dodge ram, the Packard cormorant or the ship's wheel of the later Clipper, and Pontiac even put a light in the stylized head of its namesake's hood ornament. Most American automakers, however, opted for a creative interpretation of a fifties space-age jet or rocket.

Note: All prices are in US dollars except where noted.

Published by Key Books
An imprint of Key Publishing Ltd
PO Box 100
Stamford
Lincs PE9 1XQ

www.keypublishing.com

The right of Norm Mort to be identified as the author of this book has been asserted in accordance with the Copyright, Designs and Patents Act 1988 Sections 77 and 78.

Copyright © Norm Mort, 2023

ISBN 978 1 80282 774 3

All rights reserved. Reproduction in whole or in part in any form whatsoever or by any means is strictly prohibited without the prior permission of the Publisher.

Typeset by SJmagic DESIGN SERVICES, India.

Contents

Introduction 4

Chapter 1   1950 – A New Decade of Hope 8

Chapter 2   1951 – The Hope Begins to Fade 16

Chapter 3   1952 – The Industry Adapts to Changing Times 28

Chapter 4   1953 – More Anniversaries and Change 33

Chapter 5   1954 – Slow Year and Fast Changes 41

Chapter 6   1955 – The Market Grows, the Manufacturers Shrink 49

Chapter 7   1956 – More Power, More Style, More Change 58

Chapter 8   1957 – Detroit and Designers Losing Touch? 66

Chapter 9   1958 – The Year of Successes and Failures 74

Chapter 10 1959 – The Decade of Flamboyant Styling Ends and Power to the People Begins! 83

Chapter 11 Restoring and Collecting American Four-Door Family Sedans of the 1950s 91

Introduction

In the new "baby boomer" era of postwar North America, Canada began building the Trans-Canada Highway, while the USA began the development of a vast interstate highway network to accompany improved state roads between its cities and towns. Postwar prosperity allowed more young families to purchase cars, a trend that accelerated when city dwellers moved to a perceived better life in the suburbs.

Of course, living in the suburbs encouraged people to buy a second family car, especially given that public transportation was slow to respond to the building boom in the new satellite housing developments. Besides, fuel was inexpensive. With companies also abandoning city cores to build on the fringe areas, driving to work each day was becoming a necessity, making a second vehicle a requirement for the household to function.

At the same time, Americans were taking more holiday vacations, going camping and fishing, and driving to resort locations. As a result, there was a growing demand for more functionality, reliability and comfort in American automobile designs, to carry all the family in comfort, plus their luggage, camping and fishing gear, and haul boats and trailers the longer distances to state parks all over the country.

The new four-door family sedans with their three-box design and large trunks were the perfect answer. At this point, the traditional American wooden station wagons, although practical haulers, were far too expensive and required higher maintenance.

Following the Great Depression and World War Two, there ensued a North American-wide, pent-up demand for new cars and, by the fall of 1948, automobile production was back to record levels in both the USA and Canada. In the calendar year 1945, total motor vehicle production in Canada was 132,645 units, but by 1948 that figure had nearly doubled to 263,760 units. While trucks accounted for nearly 100,000 of that production total, passenger cars reached 166,819 automobiles, of which 54.9 percent were four-door sedans; two-door sedans came a distant second at 24.4 percent. In 1949, passenger car sales in Canada continued to increase to 193,556 vehicles, of which four-door sedans now comprised 58.1 percent of the closed body types. Canada was a microcosm of what was happening south of the border, where production totals were increasing to figures once inconceivable.

Once the immediate postwar peak in demand had been satiated, the new decade beckoned and sales continued to increase, thanks to growing prosperity in both the USA and Canada. A consistent flow of fresh, modern car designs was now appearing at regular intervals, which was built on in the 1950s with

I took this photograph back in the early 1990s at a small country wrecking yard. At that time, there was little interest in collecting 1950s four-door sedans. Only pristine, original examples survived, but often those too were stripped for parts and then scrapped. Fortunately, times have changed, and while the high prices for coupes, hardtops and convertibles have conspired to force some enthusiasts to look at four-door sedans, the market itself has adapted too. Today, the family four-door sedan is seen in a new collectible light.

The American four-door family sedans of the 1950s provided passenger comfort for six, with full-size bench seats front and back. The large trunks easily handled picnic lunches, a card table and folding chairs. The cars of the 1950s were also far more reliable than hitherto, and the new state highways, along with an increased number of paved roads in general, allowed for faster, long-distance travel. Picnics and camping became very popular weekend outings and holidays. Here the 1954 Pontiac Chieftain sedan's open trunk not only offered shade, but a place to sit for the seven-year-old author and his father (Bill), mother (Edith), and the older great aunt and uncle sitting in comfort on modern 1950s aluminum and nylon folding chairs or the old 1930s wood and cloth design.

the onset of the annual major facelift in design, as well as the trend to introduce completely new models at least every three years. The pantheon of full-size sedans would soon find themselves joined by a less expensive, but practical "compact" four-door sedan.

No other decade enjoyed such immense change in engineering, design, safety, and styling, especially after beginning with great conservatism. Evolution saw the creation within just ten years of some of the most stylistically flamboyant and uniquely equipped sedans in automotive history.

For the most part, the corporate automobile showrooms of the 1950s were far less elegant and stylish than those that exist today. While some of the "Big Three" (General Motors, Ford and Chrysler) showrooms in major cities were block-sized, multi-storey buildings, providing for the viewing of the full range of models, many of the smaller independent manufacturers' line-ups were sold out of one-car showrooms that, to survive, doubled as garages and service stations. Still, even the "Big Three" had similar smaller dealerships in order to sell their cars and trucks in the many small towns across the continent.

A common ploy to attract buyers was to display brightly colored, high-styled convertibles or two-door hardtops. Many a young family flocked to the showroom with their hearts set on the flashy convertible, only to succumb to the practicality and economic reality of the family four-door sedan. Nonetheless, these sedans still came with all the color, chrome, power, comfort and the latest options and standard features. Typical of the time, friends and neighborhoods often envied those with brand new cars. Owning any new car in the fifties conveyed an image of success and prestige, which led to the coining of the phrase, "Keeping up with the Joneses." As well as being broadly aspirational, American culture of the 1950s presented outwardly as conservative in nature and the male was viewed as the head of the family. American society regarded the family man as a responsible, sensible individual in his four-door sedan, compared to those high-flying, care-free playboys in their glitzy convertibles or hardtops.

While the diaphanously clad American women standing alongside the latest model in advertisements were often dressed to look as glamorous as the automobiles unveiled, manufacturers were well aware of the practical influence that women had on sales in the marketplace. Mindful of female customers' contributions to helping choose the family's next car, or at the very least selecting its bodystyle, options, and colors, manufacturers evolved special models and options specifically designed for female buyers. In extreme cases, this went as far as Dodge offering a two-door La Femme model fitted with special vinyl patterns and colors, along with standard accessories ranging from color-matched lipsticks to purses.

Left: At the same family picnic, my sister (Eleanor) hams it up for the camera in front of our '54 Pontiac, mimicking a typical female modelling pose so common in the 1950s, albeit adding a cigar!

Below: The American auto manufacturers knew that stylish convertibles and hardtops would make good eye candy, and their press kits always featured these models. For 1954, Ford of Canada photographed that model year's new Meteor Richelieu convertible at its Oakville, Ontario plant. However, in the background are the company's volume sellers – a full row of new Ford and Meteor four-door sedans.

While some of the novel ideas and options would become mainstays, others like an optional electric shaver fortunately fell by the wayside.

For automakers, this was an era of marketing experimentation and today, some fifties designs are still admired for their uniqueness, though other attempts were just plain laughable. The truth of the old axiom, "It seemed to be a good idea at the time…' is unquestionably obvious in 1950s automotive design. Worldwide, the 1950s were also a decade of automotive takeovers and mergers involving the once globally powerful American automotive industry. Along with the traditional American "Big Three" in

Introduction

the 1950s, other smaller, but still important, manufacturers included Kaiser-Frazer, Studebaker, Packard, Willys, Nash, Checker and Hudson.

In and of themselves, the "Big Three" were composed of multiple divisions. General Motors marketed four-door family sedans in its Buick, Cadillac, Chevrolet, Pontiac, and Oldsmobile divisions; Ford in its Ford, Lincoln, Edsel, and Mercury units in the USA and the Meteor and Monarch in its Canadian divisions; and Chrysler under its Chrysler, Imperial, Plymouth, DeSoto and Dodge banners.

While not every four-door family sedan sold over the decade is pictured, I have attempted to provide a comprehensive sample of the wide array of model ranges and trim levels from every manufacturer and its divisions across each price range. This was accomplished via the use of original press photographs, period advertisements, factory brochures, owners' contributions and my own photographic collection of original and restored examples.

Interestingly, while many of the American car magazines of the 1960s focused on the sportier, high-performance cars to be found in the decade, their 1950s counterparts concentrated on family four-door sedans. Some of the magazines were, first and foremost, how-to publications concerning electronics, boats, tools, handyman projects, stories and repairs, while also containing small sections with automotive news and one or two road tests.

These four-door sedans of the 1950s were designed for transporting the family in style, comfort and convenience. Today's enthusiasts and collectors with families can do the same, with the added pleasure of driving a "classic" high-style sedan.

Above left: Of all the full-size car models built in the 1950s, the icon of the decade is the 1957 Chevrolet. It is one of the tri-Chevs (1955, '56 and '57) that enjoy a fanatical collector following dating back decades. The 1957 is preferred because of its overall styling, and in particular due to its distinctive fins. In 1957, this full-size Chevrolet was offered in three trim models; the base model was the 150, the mid-range was the 210, and the top of the line was the Bel Air, as pictured here with the more conservatively styled '55 in the background. Each line bore distinctive stainless-steel side trim and badges. Interestingly, Ford's full-size models outsold Chevrolet in 1957 despite the latter marque's immense popularity in the decades that followed.

Above right: The February 1951 issue of *Popular Science* featured a 1951 Plymouth four-door sedan on its cover. This was a rare occurrence due to the broad scope of the magazine, but Indianapolis 500 winner Wilbur Shaw was the road tester. Like most advertising in the immediate post-World War Two era, illustrations were favored over costly color photography, while inside, it was all black and white photography and illustrations.

Chapter 1

1950
A New Decade of Hope

After the Great Depression of the 1930s, followed by war, the North American automotive industry, like everybody else, looked forward to a new decade of hope.

Technology had advanced in leaps and bounds in the 1940s, which led to the 1950s being dubbed variously as the Atomic Age, the Jet Age and the Modern Age. The fifties were also the "boom years." There was the Baby Boom (with an average of four million babies born per year throughout the fifties in the USA alone), the Suburban Boom and the Economic Boom. It was the decade of rock n' roll, high-volume production, more leisure time, world airlines and the start of the computer age. Yet, for America, it was also a decade of civil unrest, seeing the rise anew of the Ku Klux Klan, the Cold War, the McCarthy-era Red Scare and the Korean War of 1950–53. In the automotive sector, the rise and fall of the independent automakers was accompanied by the growth and ultimate domination of the "Big Three."

The decade began with record sales in North America. In Canada alone, 1950 was the second year in succession that sales totals exceeded all former records. In that calendar year, 284,076 passenger cars would roll off the assembly lines, of which 60 percent, or 171,448, were four-door sedans. Across the border in the USA, meanwhile, passenger car production likewise increased by nearly 1.5 million units to 6,665,863, their buyers inspired by reduced prices. While some of the independent makes saw sales begin to falter after the immediate postwar boom, the "Big Three" remained healthy.

Back in 1925, the average car was scrapped after just 6.5 years and 25,750 miles. By 1950, according to the American Automobile Manufacturers Association, that figure had increased to 13.5 years and 116,500 miles.

Most of the new-for-1950 models appeared in showrooms in the fall of 1949. One such manufacturer to take advantage of this ultimately universal marketing strategy was Oldsmobile, which in February 1950

As part of General Motors, Chevrolet, Buick, Pontiac, Oldsmobile and Cadillac shared components, bodies and some basic engine blocks, but each division was run with its own management, designers and engineers. The closest divisions were Chevrolet and Pontiac, but even these had distinctive and unique differences. For example, they shared notchback and fastback bodies, but were quite different in specifications.

produced its three millionth vehicle (by comparison, 25 million vehicles had been produced by Chevrolet by the same year). This year was when the American automobile industry lost Ransom E. Olds, who had founded not only Oldsmobile, but also REO (on a smaller scale, Olds was also the inventor of the first motorized lawnmower). Though REO fell away in the 1970s, Oldsmobile would just survive into the 21st century. The company simultaneously discontinued its six-cylinder engine to focus on its new Rocket V8.

With increasing vehicle traffic, more roads and higher speeds, awareness of automobile safety – or lack of it – was becoming an issue. Though the mandatory wearing of seatbelts, not to mention the influence of Ralph Nader, was some way off, Nash offered seatbelts for the first time in 1950, undoubtedly saving the lives of considerable numbers of families. Gas mileage was also an issue with many buyers, and Nash covered both points in its ads, stating that the "All-welded Airflyte Construction makes the Nash safer and smoother riding by far – and savings on gas (more than 25 miles a gallon at average highway speed) make a big difference in the family budget!"

The Chevrolet Styleline and fastback Fleetline four-door family sedans were fitted with the 216ci six or 235ci six when hooked to Powerglide automatic transmission. Chevrolet and its slightly upmarket Pontiac sibling provided reliable, economical family transportation at an affordable price, and in 1950 Chevrolet achieved an industry production record of 2,108,273 units.

Dodge's all-new 1949 Wayfarer, Meadowbrook and Coronet received mild facelifts front and rear and had their trim updated for 1950. The styling was conservative compared to most of the competition, but the market liked the look. The 103hp, 230ci six-cylinder Meadowbrook and Coronet four-door sedan production totaled 221,791 of the 350,000 Dodges built. This particular 123.5in-wheelbase Coronet Special Deluxe was painted with white doors to pose as a period police car in movies.

Automatic transmissions were becoming popular and Packard's Ultramatic was standard in its Custom Eights but optional throughout the rest of its 1950 line-up. Its perceived status as the best automatic transmission in the industry saw the rights to certain components sold in succeeding years to both General Motors and Borg-Warner.

With an automatic transmission, a heater, more comfortable interior, and better tires and roads, it was even easier to enjoy driving the family to town and around the countryside in a four-door sedan.

Despite Ford Motor Company's herculean efforts filling government military contracts during World War Two, the company entered peacetime in dire financial straits. While the new 1948 Ford pickup truck was a sales success, Ford desperately needed its all-new 1949 cars to restore the company's fortunes and automotive leadership in America. Here, brothers Benson, Henry II and William Ford are rightfully pleased with this model of the 1949 four-door sedan. Only very minor trim changes were made in 1950.

Ford of America built 77,888 four-door Deluxe models and 247,000 Custom versions in 1950, but these family sedans were outsold by the trending two-door models. Some families preferred a two-door as they felt these were safer with young children in the back who might play with the door handles. Pictured in the late 1980s is a "custom" Custom being rebuilt to authentic fifties style with canted quad headlamp treatment. American four-door family sedans of the period are often fully "customized," to be enjoyed and admired today.

In 1950, Nash noted, "In this big (112in-wheelbase) Nash Statesman Airflyte (introduced in 1949), there's room for grownups, and kids, with plenty left over for Rover (under the car) - and the largest luggage compartment you ever saw!" The shape provided maximum room inside; so much so, that Nash took advantage of the new camping and touring craze by designing a "motel-on-wheels" interior. The company's advertising and brochures bragged, "So much room inside the car, the seats turn into Twin Beds in twenty seconds." Even larger was the similarly styled 121in-wheelbase Ambassador.

The following three images are from a full-page Packard advertisement of October 1949 that boasted about its new Ultramatic Drive automatic transmission, which it felt to be the best on the market. Packard noted that, with no clutch and no downshifting for hills, there was, "Nothing to learn. Just set the lever at 'H', step on the gas, and steer." Most Packard models seen today are black, but at the time a bright red was offered, which accentuated the lines of its curvaceous bodywork.

Priced at $2,635, a Packard sedan was aimed at a management-level professional who could afford an upmarket four-door family sedan. The 120in-wheelbase Packard could easily accommodate four young kids in the back seat and another up front between mom and dad. Despite Packard's earlier 1948 restyling, the company had gone from the largest prewar "independent" carmaker to the smallest. Once a leader in the luxury car field, Packard had also lost that status to Cadillac, Lincoln and, to some extent, Chrysler. All hopes would thus be pinned on the fresh, new '51 Packard that would appear early in August 1950.

Packard introduced its first all-new model in 1948; a year before its 50th (Golden) Anniversary. The fresh "bathtub" styling of the new Packard was considered handsome by many, but some critics referred to it as a "pregnant elephant." Little was changed in 1949, but sales were the second best in the company's history. Even less was changed in 1950, with some '49s re-titled with sold as 1950 models, along with leftover gold-painted anniversary editions. By 1950, however, sales had become so poor that Packard was reduced to working a three-day week, and a two-week strike in August didn't help. The earlier grille and small parking lights indicate that this particular 1950 Packard Super Eight four-door sedan was an early retitled 1949 model. An egg-crate grille distinguished the two, although this was rarely noted in Packard literature. The key difference of the authentic 1950 model was the new 327ci 8-cylinder engine with hydraulic valve lifters.

Plymouth was the third best-selling car in America in 1950. Style-wise, little was changed from 1949, the 118.5in-wheelbase sedan being offered in DeLuxe and Special DeLuxe trim. Reportedly, in some export markets Dodge and DeSoto dealers sold these models under the name Diplomat or Kingsway. Powered by a 97bhp 217.8ci L-Head six-cylinder engine, this Special DeLuxe featured additional trim and a richer-looking interior including armrests, a clock and a cigar lighter. Nearly 325,000 four-door sedans were built.

The Pontiac Silver Streak Chieftain four-door sedan was offered in two guises. The Series 25 was fitted with an in-line head 239.2ci six, while the Series 27 came with an in-line head 268.4ci eight-cylinder engine. Optional was the Hydra-Matic transmission.

The wheelbase on all of Pontiac's models was 120in. Pictured is the Silver Streak with its notchback roofline. Also offered was a fastback version of the four-door sedan, designated the Streamliner. A Pontiac was always a little fancier inside and out and, mechanically, slightly more sophisticated than a Chevrolet. It was GM's corporate vision that the Chevy owner would first move up the line to a Pontiac, then an Oldsmobile or Buick, until ultimately affording a Cadillac. Many a Chevrolet owner also had the same view, or dream!

Studebaker unveiled its all-new Raymond Loewy 1947 models in June 1946. Studebaker advertising quantified this; "From the gleaming aerocurve front end to those vigorously flight-streamed rear fenders..." The better-trimmed Champion, the Regal DeLuxe, cost $1,676. Although appealing to the low price field, Studebaker interiors were well appointed. The 113in-wheelbase Champion Regal DeLuxe four-door sedan was "...richly fitted and appointed. It's decorator styled – has foam rubber seat cushloning – luxurious upholstery."

Many a child stretched out on that sofa-like back seat and fell asleep on the late-night drive home, to be carried up to bed by mom or dad.

1950: A New Decade of Hope

The Land Cruiser ($2,287) was the top model offered by Studebaker, while the entry-level model was the Champion and the Commander a mid-range alternative. The Commander and Land Cruiser models were powered by a 94hp, 226ci six-cylinder engine. As well as better trim, the larger Land Cruiser featured a panoramic one-piece windshield.

By 1950, the Jet Age was all the rage in design, hence the jet engine-nacelle nose and aerospace-inspired hood ornament. How cool it would have been to drive a Studebaker four-door family sedan while conjuring up images of Buck Rogers in his spacecraft? In 1950, a total of 163,307 Studebaker four-door sedans were sold out of the 320,884 vehicles it built. Painted headlamp bezels were a concession due to the Korean conflict, but not on the early production, top-of-the-line Land Cruiser.

Chapter 2
1951
The Hope Begins to Fade

In 1951, US passenger-car production dropped dramatically for the first time since World War Two, falling by over 1.3 million units to 5,338,435. The Korean Conflict, as it was originally called, was quickly impacting on the supply of materials such as copper, zinc, nickel, tin and rubber. Material shortages caused temporary factory closures, and even spare tires were removed for a time in 1951. At the end of 1951, the US government relaxed these overly stringent restrictions, but these would later be re-introduced.

Another impact on production was the associated call on American automakers to devote factory car lines to military contracts. If that wasn't enough, during 1950, instalment credit had been tightened for new and used cars to 15 months, with a mandatory one-third down payment. A simultaneous nationwide rail strike certainly didn't help the supply of parts.

As in the year prior, some 1951 models had been introduced in the previous fall. This included the V8 engines and automatic transmissions on Studebaker models. Rival independent Nash, meanwhile, unveiled a one-piece curved windshield and plastic-insulated wiring to better combat moisture. For its own part, Buick introduced tinted glass, Ford offered the Fordmatic and Merc-O-Matic automatic transmissions. Safety dash crashpads were introduced on Kaiser models and Chrysler unveiled its first, all-steel station wagon. All Cadillacs were now sold with Hydra-Matic transmission, with a new instant-acting reverse control.

Two-door "convertible hardtop" models swept through the industry, appealing to the younger, style-conscious customer or successful business buyers who appreciated the sportier

Customizing and "hopping-up" your car might traditionally have been a Detroit thing, but California was the hotbed in the fifties. As well as being home to some of the USA's most legendary customizers, it was the source for thousands of aftermarket parts, kits and panels. Although the prices seem silly today, $14.95 put a lot of clothes on your family's backs in 1950.

look. Although popular, the hardtop had little influence on those who needed a more practical four-door family sedan.

The UK imported only 243 passenger cars from Canada in 1951, but demand in Belgium saw 23,393 arrive. All the same, the 1951 London Auto Show was featured in *The Autocar* of 10 November 1950, which noted, "This year's London Show marked a notable change on the part of American manufacturers. In the past Lincoln had adhered strictly to the policy of showing their domestic dealers the new models first, since export sales had only been a tiny proportion of their output. Yet, this year the 1951 Lincolns were rushed to London weeks in advance of their first appearance in the United States, and the new Studebakers are on show before most of the people in America had seen them."

Kaiser-Frazer, with its fresh designs of 1947, had initially sold well in North America, but by the turn of the decade was suffering sales falls as significant as those of the "Big Three". The company rebounded with the 1950 sales boom, but in 1951 Joe Frazer departed the scene, along with the slow-selling car bearing his name.

By 1951, with the expansion of suburban living, 12 percent of the population of the United States owned more than one automobile. Then again, the USA produced 72 percent of the world's motor vehicles in that year. Four-door sedan production in the USA fell from 3,246,996 in 1950 to 2,712,256 in 1951, but that was still a million more than two-door sedans and coupes. Automobiles were used for family vacations by 88 percent of owners and 92 percent used them for work or shopping. Other interesting automobile figures recorded in 1951 included the fact that 59 percent of city driver trips were for the purpose of making a living. A further study showed that dependency on cars increased as an American city decreased in size.

In America, the automotive aftermarket was booming, with customizing being a new trend that broke out of the chic bravura of sunny California. Even the mundane family four-door could garner its fair share of stares when sporting fender skirts, custom wheel discs, a spotlight and and external sun visor. As the decade progressed, the teenagers in the family thought bobby socks, T-shirts, jeans, that new "rock and roll" music and custom cars were "cool."

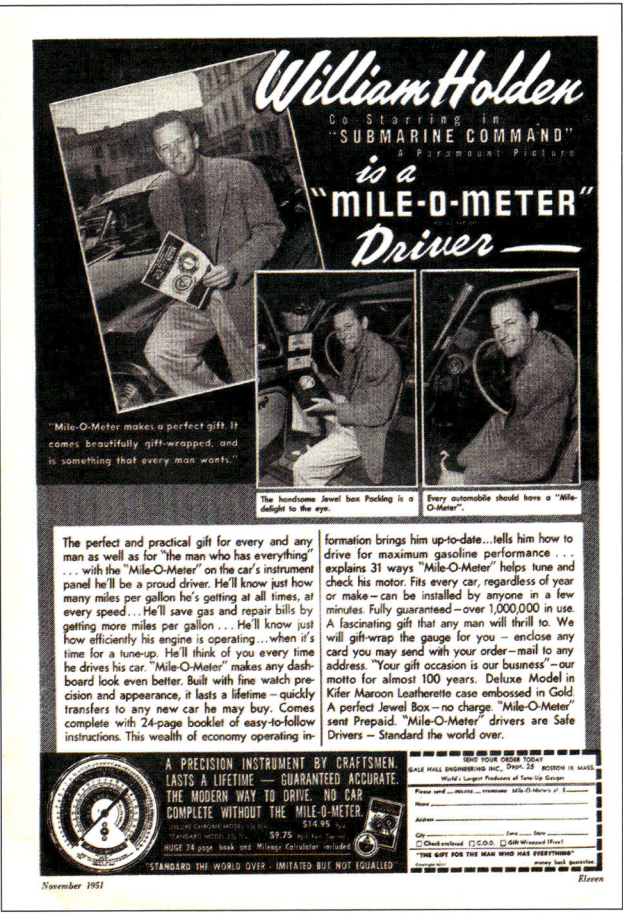

Maximizing miles/kilometres per gallon/litre has always been important to drivers and even more so to the parents of a growing family. Over a million Mile-O-Meters were apparently sold for just $14.95, and with it, you also received a 24-page booklet on saving money. In the 1950s, any amount of money saved impacted on what went on the dinner table for supper. Even a big Hollywood star like William Holden driving his Packard sedan could see that!

General Motors placed a full-color, two-page illustrated ad in magazines, promoting a cross-section of models from its divisions. This illustration supposedly depicts a typical, busy American Main Street. Everyone appears prosperous, and those families with a new Cadillac, Buick, Chevrolet, Pontiac or Oldsmobile look very happy.

In 1951, Buick offered a full range of four-door sedans that included the Special and Super Tourback and the Super and Roadmaster Riviera. This Super 8 was one of 10,000 delivered, out of a total of over 152,000 four-door sedans Buick built that year.

In 1951, Chevrolets received new brakes and a restyled front and rear end. The base model Chevrolet Styline Special was often fitted with just one option – a radio. A total of 36 percent of US radio production was installed in automobiles in 1951. Only 63,718 Stylines were built in 1951 compared to 380,270 Deluxe versions. The Chevrolet Styleline DeLuxe sedan provided a little more pizzazz inside and out, yet still provided solid, economical family transportation and comfort for five adults. Two points worth noting are the different ways the manufacturers spelled De Luxe and the fact that artistic license was never discouraged from making a car look lower and longer.

Right: The interior of this 1951 Chevrolet family sedan appears almost living-room spacious, with its huge bench seat, and a steering wheel and column almost as high as the windshield. (Artistic license again!) That said, it was nicely trimmed in cloth and vinyl, and was fully carpeted with lots of shiny chrome trim. Here, the children ride happily alongside mom on the front seat. 1950s safety didn't usually include seatbelts or even a padded dash; still, the Jumbo-Drum hydraulic brakes were a step in the right direction.

Below: Today, the Chevrolet Fleetline four-door sedan looks far more stylish and sporty than it did in its day. The hunchback/fastback look dated back to the late 1930s so, 20 years later, buyers often thought it looked old-fashioned. The newer three-box style provided more trunk space while placing the rear seat passengers ahead of the rear axle and wheels, for increased comfort and a better ride overall. A total of just 3,364 Fleetline Specials were sold, while 57,693 DeLuxe models were built.

Largest brakes in the low-price field!

No other low-priced car can match the eleven-inch diameter of Chevrolet's new Jumbo-Drum brakes. The simple design and sturdy construction make adjustment easy and help to insure positive operation at all times. The entire brake mechanism is *sealed* against dirt and mud.

THE FLEETLINE SPECIAL 4-DOOR SEDAN
Also available in the De Luxe model

Wilbur Shaw says...

"It's hard to describe this new Chrysler without going off the deep end!"

Here's why America's most famous driver picked Chrysler to pace the 1951 Indianapolis 500 Mile Race... as recorded on tape during his first drive in our beautiful new car.

"It's a whale of an automobile... the most powerful—and probably one of the fastest stock sedans manufactured in the U. S."

"It's pretty hard to describe this car without going off the deep end!"

"This engine... (the revolutionary new 180-horsepower Chrysler FirePower Engine)... I can't get over the amount of power and snap...!"

"That makes a lot of automobile in one package... In fact, I think so much of this car that I've selected it as the pace car in the 1951 Indianapolis 500 Mile Race."

* * *

Remember... the above words are Wilbur Shaw's own, reported on a tape recorder in the car. Your own reactions will be equally enthusiastic. With the revolutionary new FirePower Engine—with Hydraguide, the first power steering in a passenger car—with Oriflow Shock Absorbers that double your comfort on rough roads—Chrysler brings you the most thrilling developments in the automobile in many years. Your nearby dealer will be happy to let you feel these new thrills for yourself.

"As astonishing as the performance of this engine is, it's only half the story! The rest is power steering... (Hydraguide, an exciting new Chrysler first)... the first on any U. S. passenger automobile, and a new Chrysler Fluid-Torque Drive."

"This steering combined with the automatic transmission... is the nearest thing to an automatic pilot for a car I can imagine."

Mr. Shaw's comments are reprinted through the courtesy of POPULAR SCIENCE Magazine.

CHRYSLER
finest engineered cars in the world

It became highly popular in the 1950s for auto manufacturers to feature celebrities and race-car drivers to endorse their cars in advertising. Wilbur Shaw, winner of the Indianapolis 500 in 1937, 1939 and 1940, was recognized as a pioneer in automotive writing, but sadly died in 1954 at just 51. The 180hp, 331.1ci V8 1951 Chrysler four-door sedan was thus described by Floyd Clymer of *Popular Mechanics* (September 1951): "After beating the new V8 over all kinds of roads in every conceivable test, I'll say Chrysler has come up with a 'toughie.' I abused it and tried to find the 'bugs,' but I found none of consequence. I couldn't make it heat, rattle or squeak." Fellow automotive journalist Tom McCahill declared the 1951 Chrysler V8 as, "...the dazzlingest rattle of all."

In 1951, Ford Motor Company built 54,265 Deluxe four-door sedans and 232,691 of its Custom models as featured here. Families were willing to pay for more than basic four-door transportation, so Ford began offering an ohv, 95bhp, 6-cylinder engine along with its long-running, 100bhp Flathead V8 in 1951. Many owners found the new six-cylinder engine powerful enough both for family driving and light towing needs. As well as the sedan's spacious trunk, roof racks were a common way to carry bicycles, a canoe or a large box to hold extra luggage, a tent, and other camping gear.

For 1951, Hudson introduced its soon-to-be-legendary 124in-wheelbase Hornet in the highly touted "step-down" design. This Hornet, with its powerful and reliable 145bhp, 308ci straight-six-cylinder engine, set track records and dominated stock car racing. In a *Motor Trend* road test of March, 1951, it was noted as the fastest car tested so far, with a top speed of 97.51mph. Excellent performance, ride, handling, and comfort helped boost model year sales to 131,915 Hudsons -10,000 more than the year before. It would be the last time Hudson sales topped 100,000; a lack of development funds for modernizing the vehicle range would eventually take its toll on what was one of America's best-handling sedans.

Classic American Sedans of the 1950s: The Four-Doors

First introduced in 1950, the medium-priced, family-size, 120in-wheelbase (6½in shorter than previous models) Hudson Pacemaker was offered only in a Custom model in 1951. It was powered by a detuned 112bhp, 232ci straight six compared to the larger, top-of-the-line Hudson Commodore 8, which was equipped with a 128hp 254ci, inline eight. The 1951 calendar year saw Hudson sales fall, putting the company in 15th spot in the overall sales totals. Government-imposed Korean War restrictions, labor disputes, strikes and shortages combined to cost Hudson around a month of lost production.

By 1951, aftermarket parts, interior kits, instrumentation, oils and additives and custom modifications for both the mechanicals and cosmetics were offered to owners to individualize their cars. Aftermarket items were offered via magazine advertising, specialty shops or through mail-order catalogues. The newest Kaiser had once again been designed by "Dutch" Darrin, and was described as "Anatomic Design" due to its increased head, shoulder and leg room, which in theory suited the anatomy of the human body perfectly. (These large Kaiser models would remain virtually unchanged until the company's disappearance from the North American scene in 1955 in favor of the more lucrative South American market.)

By 1951, Lincoln's greyhound mascot was long gone. In the 1950s, hood ornaments were most often jet-inspired chrome shapes. Packard, Cadillac, and Lincoln all had historic-looking family crests that had been conjured up by designers rather than deriving from actual family heritage. Otherwise, the Cosmopolitan's front end styling was far from unique, other than its Frenched headlights. Many assume that under those large sedan hoods, there is plenty of room to work on the straight six, eight or V8. While in most cases that was true, some engines, like Lincoln's 336.7ci L-Head V8, with all its ancillaries, was a tight fit.

Little changed externally, the 225in-long, 121in-wheelbase Lincoln Cosmopolitan was a handsome automobile in profile. Rear seat comfort in the luxury four-door Cosmopolitan family sedan included a generous fold-down armrest and cloth seats. While the seat wasn't the best for thigh support, there was enough footroom to stretch out and some passengers could even cross their legs. There was more than enough room for three adults, or easily four or five children. The front floor was flat, and the rear drivetrain hump not all that intrusive. The cloth and vinyl interior featured full carpeting throughout as standard fare in the '51. Even so, while safety padding was starting to appear on a couple of manufacturers' dashboards, most designers still focused on dramatic, modern designs with lots of chrome.

Back in 1992, I wrote a comparison piece on the 1951 Cosmopolitan and the then current Lincoln Continental. Both of these Lincolns were fast, with cushion-like rides. Note the differences 40 years later in overall size and height. The Cosmopolitan's spacious trunk housed the spare tire, which was not well placed for holding the maximum amount of luggage and, although the trunk was deep, you often had to crawl inside to retrieve items. When viewed from a three-quarters front or from the rear, its girth and rather overly bulbous shape was accentuated. A total of 12,279 of these Sport Sedans were built.

In North America, there were Ford Dealers and Lincoln-Mercury Dealers. Mechanically, Mercury models were always upgraded Fords, but basic styling was shared with Fords and Lincolns while emphasizing distinctive features inside and out. Here the three Ford brothers look very pleased with themselves and the latest (but final) year for this Mercury bodystyle. Of the 310,387 Mercury models built, 157,648 were four-door sedans.

Unique to Canada was the Ford-built Meteor. With its Ford-body and blended Mercury connections, it was sold through Canada's Lincoln-Mercury dealerships as the entry in the low-price category. For 1951, it bore a new, not so Mercury-like distinctive front end, side, and rear. Although the larger Mercury grille would not easily fit, the Ford grille was rejected in favor of a unique, long rectangular wrap-around grille featuring five vertical bars. All Meteors were powered by Ford's 100hp 239ci Flathead V8.

By 1950, Nash Motors was officially a division of Nash-Kelvinator Corporation and builder of the Airflyte line-up, which featured the latest "bathtub" styling then popular with some automakers. Considering the more obvious mimicking of jets' styling cues by Studebaker, Ford, and others, Nash stressed its aircraft design even more overtly. The aerodynamic-described Nash four-door family sedan line-up consisted of the 121in-wheelbase Ambassador and the similar-looking but smaller (112in-wheelbase) Statesman. Nash's advertising pitch began "Cars with the clean, fresh beauty of jet planes…"

To accentuate the new unibody design, the Nash brochure noted, "Far advanced... in the Nash the entire body and frame, girders and pillars, floor and roof, are welded inseparably into one solid, single unit. This is the new way to build automobiles – the way stratoplanes and streamlined trains are built – stronger, safer, more modern." Both models boasted a seating width at the elbow of 63in front and 61in rear. Nash powered its Ambassador with an 115hp, 234.8ci ohv six, while the smaller Statesman was fitted with an 84hp, 184ci L-head six.

Right: The new 1951 Nash Airflytes also had large, generous, six-passenger interiors designed for North American families. Perfect for inexpensive and convenient family touring and camping, the Statesman came equipped with seats that folded easily for overnight sleeping. Nash had introduced this novel idea back in 1936. Also available were optional feather mattresses and a set of nylon mesh screen windows to provide night-time fresh air for sleeping passengers, without bugs.

Below: Oldsmobile's 135hp, 303ci Rocket V8 was the only engine offered in '51. This year the 88 was the base model with the dropping of the Seventy Series six-cylinder line. The 119½in and 120in 88s retained the 1949 styling inherited from the 98 range, while the larger 122in-wheelbase 98 continued on with its 1948 design. The two lines differed only slightly with the 98's smoother rear taillight area and unique side trim.

The 1951 Super Interior—Never before has a Super series offered such a wide choice of fine fabric selections to harmonize with the broad range of exterior colors made available in the 1951 Nash Airflyte. Here are interiors of true distinction and beauty—another hallmark of Nash quality.

Classic American Sedans of the 1950s: The Four-Doors

Above: The Oldsmobile was a great family car that boasted more room inside. In 1951, Olds was seventh in overall sales with 285,615 delivered. The top seller in the Oldsmobile line was the 98 four-door sedan, finding 78,122 buyers. This brochure image of a Deluxe Holiday 98 sedan had no problems picturing a mother with babe in arms or her daughter kneeling on the front seat talking to mom as dad motored happily along.

Left: In retrospect, many historians feel Packard's failure was due to its continued emphasis on offering downmarket vehicles, rather than competing more with its traditional rivals, Cadillac and Lincoln. The all-new for '51 best-dressed four-door Packard Patrician 400 (with high compression 327ci) retailed at $3,586, while the trimmer, less chrome-laden mid-range Packard 300 (327ci), sold at $2,971, both riding on a 127in wheelbase. The best-selling model was the low price 122in-wheelbase Packard 200 series sedan (135hp, 288ci inline 8), retailing at $2,615. In March 1951, a 250 series was added. Packard production reached 100,713 units.

Above left: Indianapolis 500 legend Wilbur Shaw in his *Popular Science* magazine (February 1951) road test of the four-door, 118.5in-wheelbase Plymouth. A lowered hood, full-width front grille, superb shocks and excellent brakes impressed him, although the lack of an optional automatic transmission was a shortcoming. Overall, the 217.8ci, six cylinder-powered '51 Plymouth was, "...most of all, dependable transportation."

Above right: New for 1951 was Studebaker's 120hp, 232.6ci V8 which came standard in the Commander (pictured) and Land Cruiser. Studebaker sales otherwise slumped to 220,000 for the model year.

1951 would be the last year for the bullet-nose styling on Studebakers – hence the only mildly modified grille, but the rear-hinged "suicide" doors were still popular with a few automakers. This lower priced, 115in-wheelbase Champion was powered by the standard 169.6ci six. Today, turning your four-door sedan into a taxi cab, police or fire vehicle is another way of enjoying the hobby. Note the cab's numbers. (Image courtesy of Roger Hill)

Chapter 3

1952
The Industry Adapts to Changing Times

Historically important automobile-industry anniversaries in 1952 included both Cadillac and Nash celebrating 50 years and Studebaker marking its century. Studebaker was established as a blacksmith and wagon maker and the firm went on to build the famous Conestoga covered wagons that took America's pioneers west to California. America also honored 50 years of the US trucking industry with a special postage stamp, but, amid all this celebration, 1952 would prove to be a troubled year for the industry.

For the second year running, automobile production was forced to take a back seat to war-related production for the Korean Conflict. As well as tanks and military vehicles, the auto industry was busy building aircraft and diesel marine engines, along with electrical and weaponry components. Other materials required for warfare also caused shortages in the automobile industry. For example, many 1952 cars suffered from poor chrome to the point of peeling occurring after mere months. Above all, designated allotments of steel to the Korean Conflict restricted maximum production levels.

On the bright side, the new small Willys-Overland Motors Aero models and the Hudson Jet were introduced in the 1952 calendar year, to compete with the similarly sized Kaiser-Frazer Henry J and its subsequent Sears Allstate offspring, as well as the already established Nash Rambler models.

New innovations for '52 included a high-beam headlight dimmer from Oldsmobile, a suspended brake pedal and a new ball-joint front wheel design from Lincoln, suspended brake and clutch pedals from Ford, a dual range Hydra-Matic transmission from Pontiac, a 12-volt electrical system from Chrysler, a four-way adjustable seat from Packard, an automatic overdrive on Plymouths and a V8 engine offered

In 1952, Studebaker's dated styling became more mainstream-looking, with a horizontal "dollar grin" grille. A fresh look was required to celebrate Studebaker's 100th anniversary, but an all-new design would not arrive until 1953. Almost 30 years separate these two four-door family sedans; the old Model T Ford appears more closely related to the horse-and-carriage era, whereas the new Studebaker's only throwback are the suicide doors, redolent of the 1920s.

on DeSoto models. Customizing, meanwhile, continued to be popular with companies, making it easy on the pocketbook for do-it-yourself enthusiasts.

However, all was not rosy in the auto industry in 1952. Adding to the constrictions already caused by the Korean Conflict, a US steel mill strike lasting 55 days resulted in a slowdown in production that cost the industry an estimated 450,000 cars and trucks. A simultaneous cooling of the market resulted in car production falling well below the 1951 total by 18.7 percent. An early resulting casualty was Crosley, which since its establishment in 1939 had offered a full range of diminutive cars, but had sold more of its station wagons (estates) than any other American manufacturer in 1948 at least. It was forced to close its doors in 1952, and more American automakers were to follow.

Fifties Buicks such as this Special had a rather unique way of opening the hood. Double-hinged, it could be opened from either side. Built for only a few months, the Standard Special, probably utilizing what was left of the split front windshields, also differed only slightly in trim. This Standard Special featured the rocker trim from a Deluxe, aftermarket wheels and non-original metallic paint. Buying any restored or refurbished sedan doesn't necessarily ensure total originality, but it should guarantee instant family cruising from the first turn of the key. In today's market, many enthusiasts prefer style, safety and drivability, often over originality.

The luxurious, 4,285lb, 215in-long Buick Roadmaster four-door family sedan was the most popular model in the 1952 line-up, with 32,069 sold of the 46,443 built. While both the Super and Special models featured three front fender-side portholes, the exclusive 130.25in-wheelbase Roadmaster was graced with four. Buick was fourth overall in industry sales, with 303,745 of the 1953 models delivered.

This 1952 Chevrolet Skyline sports such options as twin mirrors, a radio, sun visor and wide whitewall tires.

Above left: This 1952 Chevrolet Styleline DeLuxe four-door sedan is mostly original, other than the paint colors and combination, assorted painted chrome and the radial tires mounted on otherwise original wheels.

Above right: A clean original interior is a great find, even if a little worn, but it all depends on how and where the old family sedan was stored over the decades. An original interior is often more highly prized than a fully restored one.

This Styleline DeLuxe retains its original 216.5ci straight six-cylinder engine, which required very little attention before returning to the road again over sixty years later. Enthusiasts admire original paint, so a degree of wear is appreciated as much as a pristine engine compartment. A popular adage in the hobby is "It's only original once!"

Of a high-profile style rare today, this four-door 1952 Kaiser Virginian DeLuxe Traveler was painted in factory Onyx and Pasadena Yellow. The Traveler was Kaiser's answer to a station wagon and represented an innovative use of the standard four-door sedan body. Total production for both the Special and Deluxe Virginian models was 5,579. (Picture by G. Woodcock, courtesy of owner Ron Good)

With its tailgate down and hatch up, the four-door 1952 Kaiser Virginian DeLuxe Traveler was transformed from a sedan into a semi-pickup truck/station wagon/sleeper. The rear seat also folded, providing an enormous amount of room for hauling. Although a novel idea, it failed to catch the public's imagination. Note the fold-down license plate, which would later be seen on British Motor Corporation Minis. (Picture by G. Woodcock, courtesy of owner Ron Good)

For 1952, Mercury offered a larger, no-frills model for the first time, ironically dubbed the "Custom." This four-door sedan sold for $2,249. Longer, and now with forward-hinged rear doors, its lowered hood resulted in the need for a simulated hood scoop to clear the air cleaner. The rear fender skirts, full wheel discs, and wide whitewalls were all added options. A very similar-looking entry-level Lincoln was a down-graded Cosmopolitan Custom, yet still cost considerably more ($3,517) since the division had abandoned the medium price class.

Nash continued its Airflyte theme with the 88hp, 195.6ci, 114in-wheelbase Statesman 40 Series, and 120hp, 252.6ci 121-inch wheelbase, Ambassador 60 Series (there was no four-door sedan in the smaller Series 10 Rambler). The Airflyte models sported all-new Italian Pinin Farina coach-built styling to celebrate the company's 50th anniversary. By 1952, Farina styling had already graced numerous prestigious marques such as Ferrari, Lancia, Cisitalia and the new Nash-Healey sports car. The Statesman and Ambassador shared the same bodywork from the cowl back, and a production total of 152,141 units helped Nash claim over 3.5 percent of the market. Built in Toronto, this Canadian Statesman was identical other than in nameplates and was powered by a slightly smaller-stroke 82hp, 172.6ci six. Tom Cahill of *Mechanix Illustrated* (September 1952) stated "Finest shock-proof ride in the world today," and proclaimed "Pinin Farina is the Rembrandt of automobile design." McCahill recorded a 0-60mph time of 15.9 seconds and a top speed of 98mph testing the family four-door Ambassador sedan.

Above left: Despite the closeness in similarity between the Chevrolet and Pontiac models, Canadian Pontiacs were built with Chevrolet bodies, as is the case with this 1953 Pontiac. Each division had its die-hard followers. The humpback Fleetline models were dropped in both divisions for 1952.

Above right: While all the interiors of GM's A-Body shared a great deal in the way of basic underpinnings, each division had its own interior materials, colors, options and model trim. The most distinctive difference was seen in the design of the dashboard, instrumentation and styling cues. This particular Pontiac Fleetleader owner has added a set of non-original seatbelts for safety reasons, which is not uncommon in a restoration considering the all-metal dashboard. The plastic tray on the top of the dash was a typical period aftermarket addition for a pipe, sunglasses, candy for the children, etc. The three-speed manual transmission, referred to as "three on the tree" sprouted from the steering column and was often favored for hauling the family trailer or boat.

Like the Commander line, the Studebaker Champion rode on a 115in wheelbase, while the larger, grander Land Cruiser claimed exclusive use of the 119in wheelbase. *Speed Age* of June 1952 recorded a 0-60mph time of 17.95-seconds and summed up its extensive test by stating, "While both the Champion and Commander have some outstanding features, the Land Cruiser has all of theirs, besides many of its own, to make it truly an outstanding automobile."

The 1952 Studebakers sold well, reaching 167,662 units and maintaining the company's ninth spot in sales. This Champion was one of 159,978 Studebaker four-door sedans sold in the calendar year of 1952.

Chapter 4
1953
More Anniversaries and Change

1953 saw both Buick and Ford celebrating 50 years in the automobile industry, while Plymouth was now a quarter of a century old. Kaiser dropped the Frazer nameplate to become Kaiser Motors Corporation, but another change would be coming when Kaiser purchased Willys-Overland Motors, Inc., (Jeep), in April 1954. In the meantime, the larger Kaiser car line was reduced in model choices and only minor changes were made in trim and specifications.

Meanwhile, GM opened a brand new 2,280-acre desert proving ground near Phoenix, Arizona, which was slightly smaller than the 3,800-acre Chelsea, Michigan facility commenced by Chrysler at the same time. Chrysler's Dodge Division offered a V8 engine, which helped make eight-cylinder engines the premier choice of power for American buyers and thus surpassed the six-cylinder engine for the first time in history. Chrysler also purchased the automotive body plants and machinery of the Briggs Manufacturing Company, which would have serious ramifications for the Studebaker-Packard Corporation.

Under its new president, James Nance, Packard returned to the luxury car field by adding a new second line along with its renamed mid-range Clipper models. Its new Caribbean sports models were also introduced, to great acclaim. Packard sales were a buoyant 90,268 units in 1953, but that was a drop in the bucket compared to the sales figures for the "Big Three."

In 1953, air conditioning was being offered on numerous makes, automatic transmissions were now offered on most models, 12-volt systems were being used in more and more automobiles and warning lights were replacing gauges. While overall sales had decreased in the previous years, buyer demand soared in 1953 and 41.3 percent more cars were built.

While four-door sedans such as the Ford pictured were family vehicles, the bodystyle was also a favorite of rental car agencies such as Avis. The significant sales to rental agencies, taxi companies, police departments and other fleet operators formed an important percentage of the overall market for automakers. The "Big Three" competed fiercely in this market and could afford to undercut the smaller independent makes.

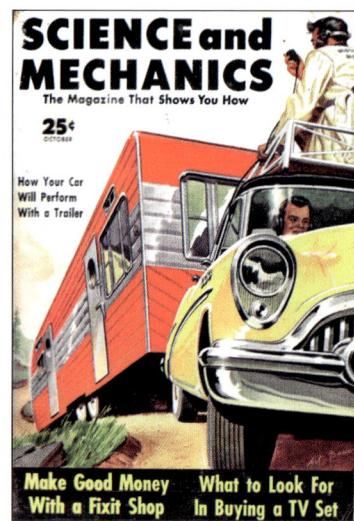 

Above left: The cover of *Science and Mechanics* (October 1953) featured a 1953 Buick Super Riviera sedan hauling a huge trailer fit for what looked like a family of a dozen or more: artistic license? All the power required would come from Buick's first V8, boasting an industry-high 8.5 compression, though Buick's straight eight was also still offered. Eighty percent of the 488,755 Buicks sold in 1953 were fitted with Dynaflow transmission.

Above right: The Chevrolet Special 150 series was sold with the 235.5ci six, plus the new one-piece windshield, hood ornament, front badge, headlamp trim and grille. Despite this entry-level model being far less fancy than the Bel Air, it still has all the styling and Chevrolet dependability, as well as club and parts support, and certainly looks the part today. Chrome paint used on the bumper and grille provide a clean, fresh look at minimal cost, but be aware that the lustre fades quickly!

The Bel Air was the highest-priced trim of a four-car, six-cylinder Chevrolet line-up in 1953. The rear fender skirts were standard, while the front bumper guard and radio were optional extras.

The 125.5in-wheelbase Chrysler Windsor Deluxe sedan was one step down from the New Yorker, but not V8 powered. Introduced in 1954, PowerFlite transmission quickly became the popular choice for these, while the 211in-long Windsor models came equipped with the L-head, 119hp, 264.5ci six-cylinder engine. The ultimate Chrysler models were the larger Custom Imperials and later Newport Imperials.

The 1953 Dodge Coronet featured the first Chrysler Hemi V8 and was soon to prove itself. With its four-door sedan stock car, Dodge became the new AAA record holder with a flying start of 102.622mph, and also whizzed to a new AAA standard of 72.325mph for a measured mile from a standing start. Dodge also scored six NASCAR wins in 1953.

The top trim level Dodge Coronet could be ordered with a six (as of March 1953) or V8, a small air scoop below the hood ornament designating V8 power. The 140hp, 241ci Hemi engine also triumphed over the competition in the V8 class in the Mobilgas Economy Run. Despite a sizeable production run, these four-door sedans are rare today.

Above left: Despite the Hudson Hornet's enviable domination of American stock-car racing, the step-down styling had aged quickly. *Science & Mechanics* of December 1952 road tested the similarly styled, smaller-wheelbase Wasp and recorded a top speed of over 101mph and a 0–60mph time of around 15 seconds. The Wasp cost $2,448, while the Hornet was priced at $2,769. Roadability was ranked "exceptionally high" on both smooth and rough surfaces, while riding comfort was termed very good on smooth roads, but not so much on rough surfaces. Overall, the Wasp's road-holding made it "…one of the most roadable American cars you can buy today," and the Hornet or Wasp are still great family sedans to own.

Above right: Costing $12m to develop, the much-anticipated Hudson Jet arrived to compete in the lower-priced small car field that the Nash Rambler had dominated since 1951. Alas, also new at this point were the small Willys and Henry J, both of which were considered more stylish. Hudson management hoped the Jet would be the answer to their prayers to save the ailing car maker, but sales were to prove very disappointing. The 104–114hp, 6-cylinder Jet was hardly step-down, stood far too tall, and its overall proportions were rather awkward looking.

The Jet's unique "Monobilt" construction method could more accurately be described as overbuilt, as it made the cars too heavy, and the bodies were built off-site. Even so, the example featured in the August 1953 issue of *Speed Age* clocked 0–60mph in 12.8 seconds and a top speed of 96mph; impressive for a small car. It recorded "…times that cannot be duplicated by many with much more muscle in the horsepower department."

This unique Meteor was popular in Canada, but total production of all models only topped 37,000 cars. A special crest with maple leaves was the most visible indicator of a Canadian model, while production overall saw a blend of US Mercury, Ford and distinctive Canada trim, engines and interior appointments. Surprisingly, a relatively high number of Meteors survives today. Many enthusiasts create taxi cab, police, or fire-chief versions out of their four-door sedans and rent them out for period films. Few moviegoers would notice the fact, however, that this particular example, with Nevada markings, was in reality a Canada-only Meteor.

Oldsmobile was one of the earliest American manufacturers to establish itself as reliable and well-built, and this reputation endured over the next half-century. The new 12-volt, 150hp, V8 1953 Olds 88 was seen and marketed as typical customers' first step up from a Pontiac, and it helped make the division a leader in the mid-price field, contributing to total sales of 334,462 cars in 1953. There were 17 solid colors and 16 two-tone shades to choose from on the 88, and for $2,126 in total you also got a restyled interior and dash. The upmarket Super 88 shown here was priced at $2,252.

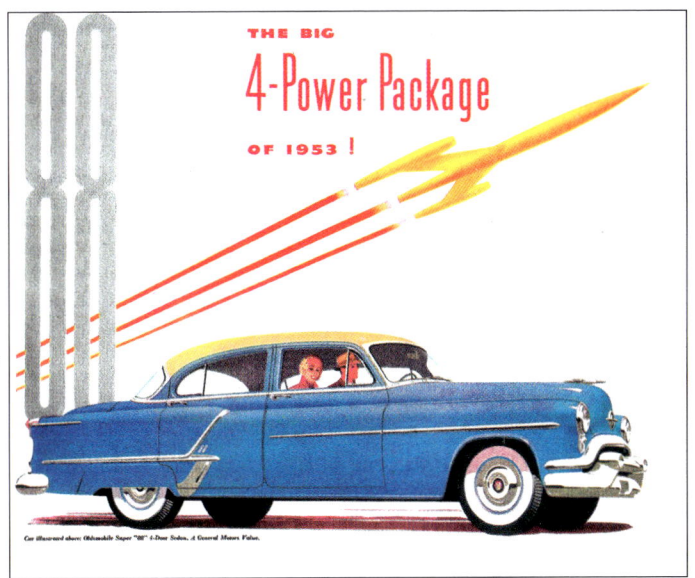

Packard's return to the luxury car arena saw the 300 become the Cavalier ($3,255), while the 400 added the Patrician model ($3,740), which also came in a new "Corporate Executive" series. The Patrician was powered by a 327ci straight eight and the Ultramatic transmission, with power steering an additional option for $190. At 7,456 units, Patrician sales in 1953 almost doubled that of the previous year.

Packard's best-selling line was its new 122in-wheelbase Clipper. Mildly facelifted, with reshaped rear fenders, a wrap-around hardtop and two-door hardtop-style rear window, and renamed from 200 the year before, the 213.1in-long four-door Clipper DeLuxe sedan sold for $2,745.

Left: This 122in-wheelbase Pontiac Chieftain Deluxe sedan wasn't as long as the artist imagined, although at over 202in, it was sleek enough. Still, it was handsome and all-new for '53. The Deluxe version had the dual chrome hood and body trim, stainless stoneguards, chrome full wheel discs and other glitz. With a choice of the 115hp, 239.2ci six or 122hp, 268.4ci inline 8 as power options, most buyers opted for the latter.

Below: In 1952, Willys re-entered the car market with the economical compact Aero, available only as a two-door sedan. The following year saw the Aero line-up expanded to include a four-door sedan and a stylish two-door hardtop. The new Aero-Falcon was powered by a more economical Lightning Six. The marque's popularity continued to increase gradually, with production in 1953 numbering 41,375 total units.

THE AERO-FALCON 4-DOOR SEDAN provides the roomy comfort of an airliner with the performance and economy of the LIGHTNING "6" Engine. There is a steadiness on curves and a surprising lack of engine vibration or wind noise with the Aero Willys thanks to its low center of gravity, low wind resistance and rubber-pillowed suspension mountings.

Above: Not sure why the owners of such a "posh" home would buy an inexpensive new Willys, but it didn't hurt the car's image. Perhaps some wealthy Americans bought their six-year-old daughters small compact cars for their birthday? All kidding aside, the interior provided big-car accommodation for six.

Right: While the two-door Studebaker hardtop's styling was considered stunning, the automaker's misguided management scheduled production of 60 percent sedans and 40 percent coupes. At only 60½in high, the four-door sedan was handsome by itself, but demand proved to be the reverse of projections and thousands of sales were lost, resulting in a slight overall drop in model year production totals. The coupes and the high-end Land Cruiser rode on a 120.5in-wheelbase, while all the other models sat on a 116.5in-wheelbase. All the Studebaker models were winners in their respective classes in the prestigious Mobil Economy Run, however; a four-door Champion sedan fitted with overdrive was the "Top Winner" with an average of 26.86mpg.

Enthusiasts buying an American four-door sedan shouldn't hesitate to add some customizing or performance modifications to remind the purists that this approach was encouraged even when new. Vintage accessories and power mods are greatly admired by serious collectors.

Chapter 5

1954
Slow Year and Fast Changes

By the time the dust had settled on the inconclusive result of the Korean War, industry sales were down by 500,000 automobiles, but 2,592,841 four-door family sedans were sold in 1954.

The boom years of 1947 and '48, followed by a number of good years in general, were a memory by now and, to survive, many of the independent automakers scrambled to merge. Nash (officially known as Nash-Kelvinator) and Hudson formed American Motors, and by the end of the year moved all production to Kenosha, Wisconsin. Studebaker and Packard simultaneously formed the Studebaker-Packard Corporation, which would also eventually close all its plants and operate out of South Bend, Indiana, other than retaining Studebaker's Canadian plant in Hamilton, Ontario. For all the decline in demand, Packard was solvent and had wanted all the independents to merge into one, but instead was left with struggling, debt-ridden Studebaker and inherited all its problems.

On the bright side, Packard was the first to introduce tubeless tires as standard equipment, yet by the end of the year every company had switched to offering them as standard. Packard also built the last of its eight-passenger, four-door limousines, while, Henney, the bespoke builder of limousines and professional vehicles and latterly supplying limousine bodies on Packard chassis, would close its doors in 1954 after completing just 35 Packard limousines and 326 Packard professional cars.

A fifties fad that was revived and copied/re-interpreted in the new millennium was Buick's distinctive porthole styling cue. Buick buyers loved them. The new Century model rode on Buick's upmarket Special chassis, and was powered by the Buick Roadmaster 195hp or 200hp, 322ci V8; production of Buick's straight eight ceased. The Buick Century was considered the fastest sedan of 1954.

While the independent automakers were either struggling or losing millions, the "Big Three" were able to invest millions in new factories, proving grounds, engines, new models, and test facilities. For instance, Ford, recovering from the Korean Conflict-imposed tooling restrictions, introduced its delayed, all-new, ohv V8.

Overall, the market was changing, with much younger buyers looking for new automobiles with high performance and lots of style. While the traditional new-car buyer demographic had been conservative in its tastes, this younger generation wanted more flash and dash – and they were about to get it. In the broadest sense, the gradual construction of more and more highways across North America, both inter-city and interstate (or interprovincial), attracted consumers to more powerful, comfortable, economical and better-handling family sedans. Many dreamed of owning the same automobiles they read about and that they saw racing in NASCAR events and on local dragstrips.

Left: At an overall length of 206in, the Century, Special and Skylark Buick four-door sedans provided plenty of room for both passengers and luggage. Comparing the Century to the Special, *Motor Trend* (October 1955) concluded, "The Special handles well, is comfortable, and even looks like a big car, yet is far from that. True, it doesn't have the snap of the Century, but you're not paying $250 for it, either."

Below: In previous years, the 122in-wheelbase Buick Special sedan design had been the most popular model, but this dropped into third in 1954 with production of 70,365 four-door units. Minimal styling changes had been made, with the biggest being the new wrap-around windshield.

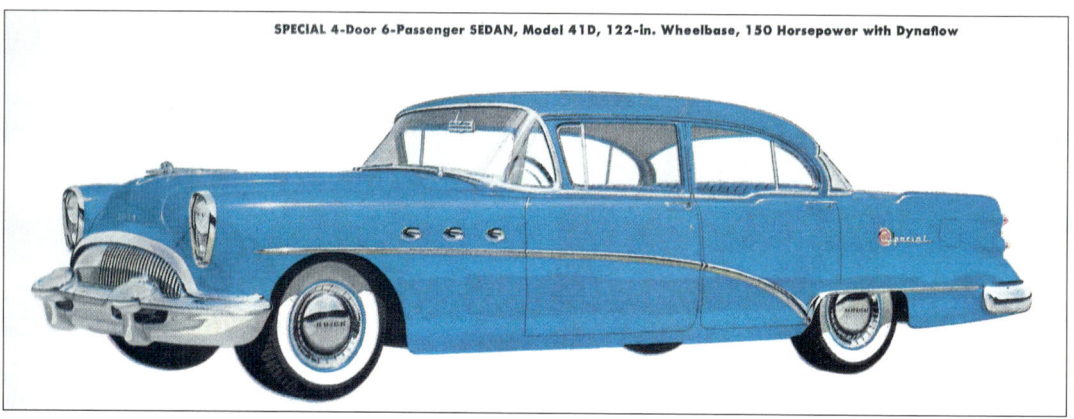

Right: At a vintage race in the 1990s, I met "Gentleman" Jim Kimberly, who was attending because his former Ferrari (pictured) was competing. Jim Kimberly was the Kimberly in Kimberly-Clark (Kleenex, etc.) The 1954 Cadillac was certainly capable of towing his Ferrari, which apparently rolled off its trailer going to an event. Tire and spark plug companies often teamed up with car companies in joint ads, which is still a common practice in the advertising industry today.

Below left: Chrysler's De Soto had its own loyal following, but competed within the Corporation with higher-priced Plymouth models, lower-priced Chrysler models and popular Dodges. New for 1954 was the De Soto Automatic, featuring full-time power steering, power brakes, no-sway ride control and the PowerFlite fully-automatic transmission. For powerplants, there was a choice of the Fire Dome 170hp V8 or the Powermaster Six. De Soto used the term "forward look" to describe its styling, which over the years and decades would be used again to describe Chrysler products. Nameplates with embossed "Firedome" or "Powermaster" legends graced the front fenders.

Below right: The interiors of the De Soto Automatic Fire Dome V8 were color-keyed to the exterior color, with the seat colors and panel pattern matching the door panels. The nylon interior featured pleated backrests and deeply set buttons, while the door hardware was of chrome finish.

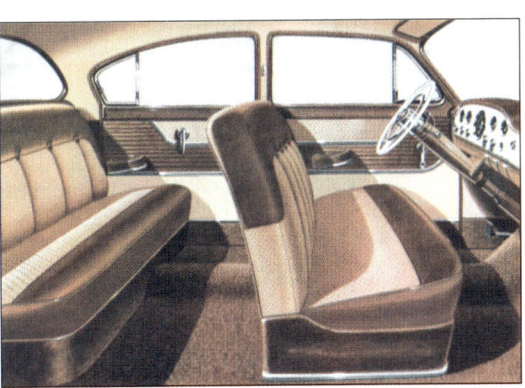

Classic American Sedans of the 1950s: The Four-Doors

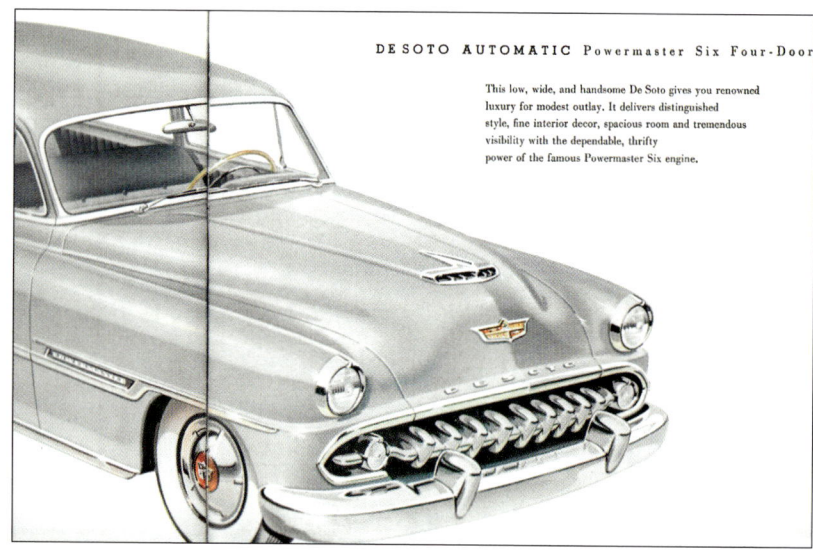

DE SOTO AUTOMATIC Powermaster Six Four-Door

This low, wide, and handsome De Soto gives you renowned luxury for modest outlay. It delivers distinguished style, fine interior decor, spacious room and tremendous visibility with the dependable, thrifty power of the famous Powermaster Six engine.

The six-passenger, four-door Automatic Powermaster sedan was described as providing "...renowned luxury for modest outlay." The interior was outfitted with "sofa-soft cushioning" upholstery in two-tone colors. A larger, eight-passenger Fire Dome and Powermaster four-door sedan was also available.

Handsomest Car Ahead!

This view of the new Powermaster Six emphasizes some of De Soto's new beauty points . . . the massive, newly-designed bumper and guards . . . beautiful swept-back fenders and big, low-slung deck lid . . . slender rear posts and a huge one-piece window . . . and lovely new combination stop light, back-up light, and turn signal clusters.

This brochure image was titled, "Handsomest Car Ahead!" Of note were the "massive" rear bumper and guards, the "beautiful" swept-back fenders, and the "lovely" tail lights. In retrospect, perhaps the wrap-around rear windows and thin C-pillars for better rearward vision, as well as the generous trunk, might have been of more importance to family buyers.

The 1954 Hudson Jet cost less at $1,858, while the Super Jet was just $1,954. A $1,621 two-door club sedan was added along with others near the end. A total of 22,143 Jets were built in 1953 and a mere 14,224 in 1954.

Above left: With its good performance and "old auntie" styling, the Hudson Jet is quite a Q-Ship. And yet, it returned an economical 31mpg at 30mph and 22mpg at 60mph. Sadly, production delays combined with labor disputes and the loss of Hudson's government contracts due to the truce in the Korean War put the automaker on the ropes financially. Stagnating Wasp and Hornet sales ultimately crashed the Jet.

Above right: The entry-level Willys four-door sedan in 1954 was the Lark DeLuxe. Most were sold powered by the Lightning F-head, 90hp, 161ci, six-cylinder engine. The Kaiser 115hp, 226ci L-head engine became the big six in the higher-priced Aero models, but could also be ordered in the Lark, making it a particularly quick sedan. *Motor Trend* (August 1953) loved the Willys except for its, "…tendency to heel-over…" and overall roadability. Today, these problems can be easily overcome with a few suspension mods to create a "pocket rocket."

Right: Despite a major facelift for 1954 and an interior praised for its use of design, colors and textures, Kaiser sales continued to decline and tumbled below 10,000 cars. It was America's only supercharged car and accelerated from 0–60mph in 13.9 seconds, with a top speed of well over 100mph.

10,000 feet up … and cruising like an airliner, thanks to its airplane-type supercharger forcing in 220 cu. ft. of air per minute at 60 M.P.H.

Only passenger car factory-equipped with a "blower"!

The only '54 car under $6000 equipped with supercharger, the '54 Kaiser's performance must be experienced to be believed.

Developed by Kaiser and McCulloch engineers, Kaiser's supercharger is controlled by a solenoid switch on the accelerator. It idles at cruising speeds (saving gas) but revs up the instant you step down on the gas.

Operating on a variable drive belt, it's geared at 4.4 to 1 to pour oxygen into its sealed carburetor. It boosts Kaiser's 118 h.p. up to a quick 140, and torque up to 215 foot pounds at 2400 r.p.m.

The result: A "bomb" that leaves other cars flat-footed at a light or on a hill. It's quiet in operation, too. Servicing is quick and easy. And it teams beautifully with Dual-Range Hydra-Matic* or Overdrive*.

Stop in at your Kaiser dealer. See a power plant that's "all muscle" not "all beef"!

*Optional at low extra cost.

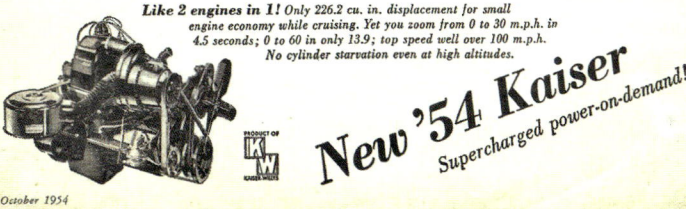

Like 2 engines in 1! Only 226.2 cu. in. displacement for small engine economy while cruising. Yet you zoom from 0 to 30 m.p.h. in 4.5 seconds; 0 to 60 in only 13.9; top speed well over 100 m.p.h. No cylinder starvation even at high altitudes.

New '54 Kaiser *Supercharged power-on-demand!*

October 1954

Despite its lower price, the Willys Aero was fitted with a decently appointed and stylish interior. In fact, Willys boasted of its "Color-Symphony Interiors." Optional equipment included air conditioning, a heater and defroster, a radio, overdrive and Hydramatic transmissions, directional signals, two-tone paint and whitewall tires.

The Willys Aero unibody design was described as a compact car with a big car interior. The front and rear seats were wide and headroom was generous. Outside, the Aero was 72in wide, 60in high and rolled along on 4.50x15 tires. Gas mileage was praised, as the six provided an average of 35mpg. In 1954, Kaiser production moved to Toledo from the old Willow plant in Michigan, which was partly responsible for Aero-Willys production dropping to a mere 11,865 cars.

Another uniquely Canadian Meteor model was the Niagara. For a stronger Canuck identity, the former names were dropped. The base model was just the Meteor, while the mid-range was dubbed the Niagara with the Rideau as the top model. The Merc-o-Matic was not offered on the base model and a $203CAD option on the others. Power was via the 125hp Mercury engine. Meteors soldiered on with the old Flathead V8s. There was a Niagara Special that featured the Ford instrument panel rather than the standard Mercury panel. A strike in Canada saw production drop to just 25,885 Meteors.

AMBASSADOR CUSTOM 4-DOOR SEDAN . . . A completely new note in luxury distinguishes the Nash Ambassador . . . with sparkling new interiors styled by Madam Hélène Rother, in rich needlepoint and long-wearing homespun fabrics.

Despite being a smaller independent, Nash sought out experts in design to produce the most modern and fashionable automobiles for North Americans to buy. Yet, despite attempting to appeal to the European roots of hundreds of thousands of new immigrants arriving in North America in the 1950s, these more sophisticated designs didn't translate into higher sales. Today, however, a Nash Ambassador Custom offers an opportunity for hobbyists to acquire a unique-looking, well-designed family four-door sedan. Though maintaining one of these poses a far greater challenge than a Chevrolet, myriad help from collectors can be sought on the internet.

Motor Trend (October 1954) summarized its road test of the Ambassador thus; "A top-notch family car with features that demand a buyer's close inspection." It also stated that "If ever a car was designed for a family that likes outdoor living and revels in taking trips, the Nash Ambassador is it." Performance-wise, the Ambassador could break 100mph, but 0–60mph took a rather leisurely 15.7 seconds. At a speed of 60mph, gas mileage recorded by the 130hp, 252.6ci six-cylinder Nash was 20.6mpg.

The 110hp, 195.6ci Nash Statesman was the less expensive, more economical model in the Nash big-car line-up, with only a minor facelift since its introduction in 1952. Custom versions included the dressy continental rear spare tire, whilst both the Ambassador and the Statesman had updated interior and dash designs. Nash sold just over 15,000 Statesman four-door sedans and over 17,500 Ambassador family sedans in 1954.

The six-cylinder 1954 Plymouth Savoy was designated as the mid-priced offering between the Plaza and Belvedere, all three being named after famous hotels. Plymouth sold 139,383 Savoy four-door sedans, making it the most popular Plymouth in '54.

Motor Trend (October 1954) also tested the four-door Studebaker, remarking on how the two-door coupes had a longer wheelbase as well as being longer overall, like the top-of-the-line Land Cruiser sedan model. They concluded their six-cylinder Champion road test by saying, "Don't take a Champion unless you are a calm, contented driver, with no aspirations to burn up the road." The Custom nameplate became the base version in 1954 for both the Champion and Commander lines, while the top-of-the-line version was dubbed the Regal. The Champion Regal was immediately recognized by a chrome spear stretching from the front door to the tail, while the mid-range DeLuxe version of the Champion (shown) was distinguishable by just the rear fender side trim. (Image courtesy of Roger Hill)

Chapter 6

1955
The Market Grows, the Manufacturers Shrink

As Cole Porter lyricized, "Oh, what a swell party this is! It's great! It's grand! It's a w-o-o-o-o-o-nder land!" No one in the auto industry was expecting a boom year in production in 1955. The total number of four-door sedans built that year was 3,043,564, which was almost twice the number of two-door and four-door hardtops. Despite the record production volumes of automobiles in the USA, one out of every eight cars on the road was still prewar but with recorded sales 44 percent higher

Above left: The "Big Three" were often featured on the covers of magazines, but conspicuous by its absence in the December 1954 edition of *Popular Science* was the all-new Chevrolet. Three of 1955's lineup were featured in a White Christmas-themed American setting, complete with happy families.

Above right: True to its name, *Consumer Reports* was a magazine that tested everything from televisions to washing machines in a matter-of-fact manner. In this particular edition, the '55 Cadillac was placed front and centre. Cadillac's most popular model at this point was the Series 62 four-door sedan, which now shared the stylish Florentine curved rear roofline first seen on the make's 1954 hardtops.

than in 1954 (and 18.8 percent better than the previous record year of 1950), inroads were definitely being made into the numbers of older vehicles. Even so, some would leave the party early.

While car sales for newly formed American Motors (Nash in particular), and Studebaker-Packard were both up, the overall picture for both wasn't, nor for Kaiser-Willys. Overall market penetration had dropped to below 5 percent for the smaller independent automakers. Kaiser-Willys offered only one full-size car, its Manhattan model, in 1955, but by the end of the year, the company dropped all its car lines, including the compact Willys.

Although Studebaker-Packard was now the fourth-largest US automaker, the corporation lost $29.7 million. Packard, whose bodies had been built by Briggs, found itself without a supplier after Chrysler bought the company. Instead, the new Conner Avenue plant in Detroit was established to build the bodies for the larger Senior Packard line. However, the inexperienced and overworked employees in the cramped space of this newly constructed line turned out cars that weren't the best quality. Dealers as well as buyers complained, resulting in many of the last loyal Packard buyers switching their loyalties to Cadillac and Lincoln. Regardless, Packard was pleased with its total of 55,247 cars sold in 1955 and had high hopes of an even better 1956.

Meanwhile, over at Kaiser, only the Manhattan model was being offered and just 1,231 sedans were built, of which 1,021 were shipped to Argentina. The tooling, etc. was then all sent to Argentina to become part of the highly successful IKA (Industrias Kaiser Argentina). The Manhattan was rebadged as the Kaiser Carabela, and these sedans would be built from 1958 to 1962. In total, almost 575,000 Kaiser, Frazer, and Willys cars were built in America; an estimated 500,000 were Kaisers, with the vast majority being four-door sedans.

In Canada, as in the USA, the four-door sedan was still the most important showroom model. In 1955 total passenger car production reached 374,945 vehicles, of which 224,973 were four-door sedans. This body style's closest rival was the two-door sedan, at just 68,919 cars. While the station-wagon market would increase significantly over the decade, at this point the handy haulers only achieved 16,843 sales. In the USA, 3,043,564 four-door sedans were produced, plus 1,677,430 two-door sedans, 1,666,984 four-door hardtops and over 750,000 two- and four-door station wagons.

Taking third place in overall sales, Buick had bumped Plymouth in 1954, but with just a facelift for '55 to combat an all-new Plymouth, the division was counting on its new variable-pitch Dynaflow transmission to handle the 236hp V8s in the Century, Super and Roadmaster models. The Buick Special was powered by the 188hp V8 and was immediately recognizable by the four portholes on its front fenders.

Right: The Century was the second most popular model of the 158,796 Buicks sold in 1955 and helped Buick lock down third place in sales again. Buick's four-door sedans were still its most popular bodystyle, yet a mere 13,269 were Century four-doors. This would herald the model's demise after sales were lost to the related four-door Roadmaster sedan.

Below: The Chevrolet Bel Air was the top-of-the-line model in 1955. All the sedans rode along on a 115in wheelbase with an overall length of 195.6in. Despite being unchanged in size, the all-new styling made the sedan appear to be longer, in part because it was lowered by 2½in. A strengthened frame and suspension changes improved ride and handling. *Popular Mechanics* described the front end styling as "Ferrari-type." Add in the all-new V8 engine and an optional overdrive, and family cruising never looked so good.

Chevrolet's base model for 1955 was the Two Ten, which was easily distinguishable at a glance by its different side trim treatment. New for '55 were features such as 12-volt electrics, tubeless tires, improved steering, a centre glovebox and suspended brake and clutch pedals. The sedan also came with a choice of three engines and three transmissions.

While the 123hp or 136hp 235.5ci six-cylinder engines might have found it a bit of a chore to haul this Porsche to races, the standard 162hp or optional 4-bbl and dual exhaust 180hp 265ci V8 would have no problem. Today, it is easy to enhance the power output, or like many, just drop in a 350ci Chevy V8 built to your specs. In *Motor Trend*'s January 1955 test, a four-door V8 Two Ten sedan with Powerglide achieved a 0-60mph time of 12.3 seconds and a top speed of over 90mph. The magazine concluded that, "The greatest compliment we could pay to this car is that our praise is so high and our criticisms so minor that we find it hard to believe it's a descendant of previous Chevrolets."

Imperial had become a separate brand in 1954, but not until 1955 did the real differences from redesigned Chrysler models emerge, heralded by unique front- and rear-end styling. The total of Imperial hardtop and four-door sedans exceeded 11,000 units, of which 7,840 were sedans. The Imperial's wheelbase was 130in, its weight 4,565lbs, and standard power was from a 250hp, 331.1ci V8.

The Chrysler New Yorker Deluxe was the top-of-the-line model. It was offered in Newport and even fancier St. Regis guises, the latter instantly recognisable by its two-tone look. It was powered by the Corporation's 250hp, 331.1ci V8. By 1955, Chrysler dominated both NASCAR and AAA-sanctioned stock-car racing by winning events with Chrysler 300, DeSoto and Dodge four-door sedans, all of which were powered by first generation "Hemi" V8 engines. Four-door sedans were the usual raceway competitors at this point in time. With nearly 20 stock-car wins plus a victory over 37 other makes in the 1955 Mexican Road Race, the Corporation flaunted its successes in motoring magazines such as *Mechanix Illustrated* (August 1955).

Described by Dodge's PR people as "flair-styled," this Custom Royal Series four-door sedan features "...a dashing hood ornament, projected headlight hoods, a New Horizon swept-around windshield, cut-back doors, flared wheel openings and a streamlined rear deck." It was powered by a Super Red Ram 183hp V8. A two-tone paint treatment accentuated the lower roofline, sloping hood and twin-jet taillight section. Mom and dad certainly seem impressed.

While new inside and out, the Ford four-door sedan was plain white bread compared to its splashy Ford Crown Victoria hardtop and less stylish than the new Chevy, but it was still a handsome vehicle with all the traditional Ford virtues. The Ford Custom (Customline) pictured was positioned between the base Mainline and the high-end Fairlane, replacing the Crestline. The Town Sedan was a Deluxe Fairlane four-door sedan. Like the Chevy, new Fords were also lower and wider, but also longer. Its less flashy styling proved popular, achieving Ford's second highest sales record since 1923 when the Model T ruled the roads.

In 1955, Lincoln was praised again for its ride and handling. With its first facelift since 1952 came a new and much improved transmission. The Capri model cost $3,752 and 10,724 were built. The rear fenders and rear end were also extensively restyled, and a Ford Turbo-Drive transmission replaced the former GM unit. The V8, meanwhile, grew to 341ci and powered-up to 225hp. For all this, it was unsuccessful in the marketplace, and Lincoln production dropped to just 27,222 units.

The unique Canadian Monarch shared much of its existence with the US-built Mercury. The full-size Monterey down to Custom line provided the body with its forward-raking headlamps and full-scope windshield, on a common body design dating back to 1951. Both the Canadian and US models were heavily chromed and shared Lincoln DNA. Monarch as a separate brand offered a choice of two V8s and added a new headline four-door sedan mid-year in the 188hp or 198hp 292ci Richelieu model. The Canadian Ford-like Meteor range offered the Niagara and Rideau models.

Oldsmobile had its most successful year in six decades, selling 583,179 cars in the '55 model year and a whopping 643,459 in the calendar year to make it the fourth highest-selling marque in the US market. This was all despite only a mild restyling, but it helped that its Rocket V8 engines increased to 185hp and 202hp. Production of the $2,362 Oldsmobile 88 four-door sedan alone totaled 57,777 units, while the Super 88 sedan achieved 111,316 units and four-door 98s sold nearly 40,000. Unique on the 98 was the optional left-hand-operated spotlight.

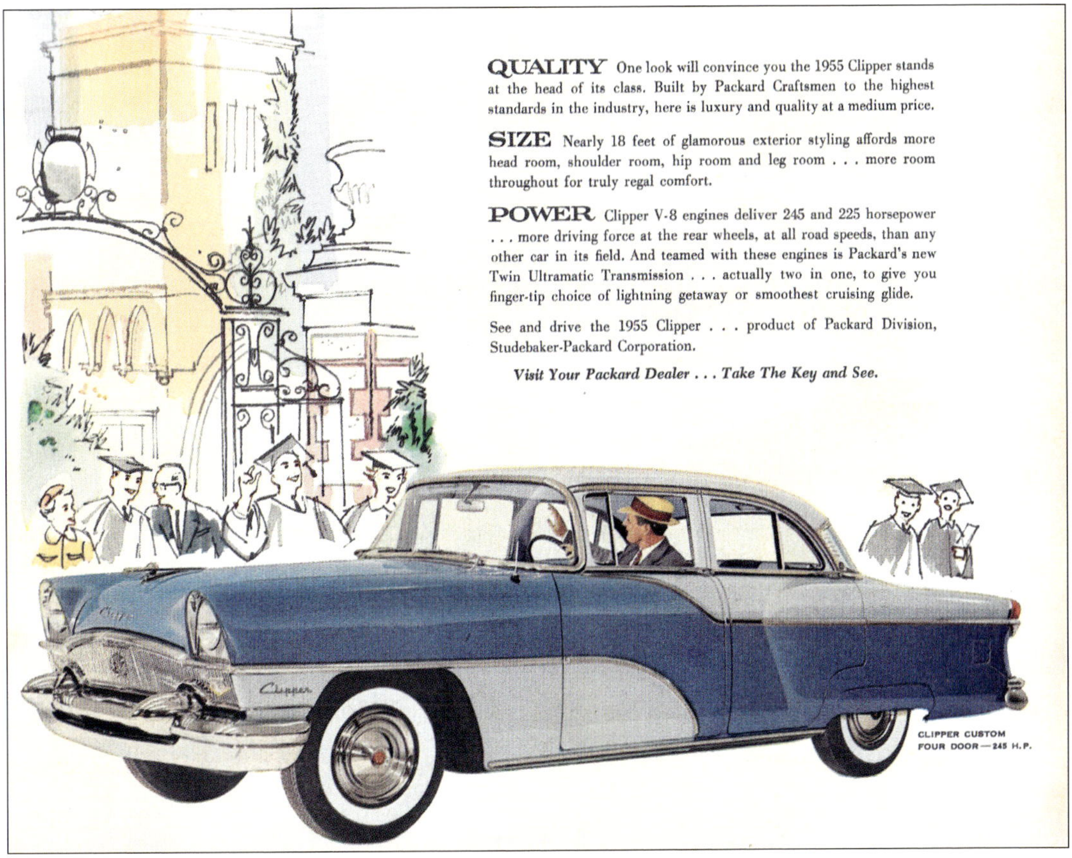

Once a leader in America's luxury car market, Packard had introduced the original Clipper in order to survive the Depression. Survival came at a high cost, however, as by the 1950s Packard was no longer associated with the finest cars in America and was now part of the Studebaker-Packard Corporation. Even the handsome new 18ft-long Clipper's days would be numbered despite the availability of two of the firm's four new V8s, its well-designed automatic transmission and torsion bar suspension. The larger Senior Packards still bore the proud crest, while the Clippers now wore a sailing ship's wheel.

This well-optioned Studebaker Commander looked very much like its lower-priced Champion sibling in 1955. The Champion sedans were once again Mobil Economy winners, and both had 116.5in-wheelbases. The bare-bones Commander Custom version was a mere $200 less than a much fancier Regal and, accordingly, was dropped in 1956. Commander models were twice as popular in 1955 than the '54 versions and outsold the Champion for the first time since 1939. A '55 Commander four-door sedan sold for $2,614.

Studebaker's simple, elegant styling was superseded by chrome-laden models in 1955. North Americans loved chrome and Studebaker fulfilled that desire. Lots of flash means lots of cash for owner/restorers today, as re-chroming these models is costly. Under the hood, the new 140hp V8 could boast the shortest stroke in the industry, at only 2.813in. Later Commanders came with a 162hp 259ci V8. In 1955, Studebaker announced price cuts on all models, bringing the Commander more in line with the low-priced V8s from Ford, Chevrolet and Plymouth.

The top-of-the-line Land Cruiser nameplate was replaced by the resurrected 120.5in-wheelbase President series. It had been rumored that the Packard V8 would be under the hood, but instead it was a new Studebaker 4-bbl 175hp V8. The four-door sedan President models consisted of the upmarket State and Deluxe. The State was first offered without the later wrap-around windshield and with the old dashboard, and also carried the older, more formally dressed interior. Rear fender skirts were standard. This example is the later version which also saw a power increase to 185hp. Two-tone paint was available at no extra cost on State models. (Image courtesy of Ed Malthaner/Digitape Designs)

Fuel economy was important, but only to some North Americans, as gas was 'cheap' in 1956 at 30c a (US) gallon. Bigger and better was the American way; in many families, compact cars would be second cars, but only until a full-size car was more affordable. A Studebaker Champion achieved 27.4mpg to win the 1955 Sweepstakes Trophy.

Chapter 7

1956
More Power, More Style, More Change

This year, the US Congress initiated the Federal-Aid Highway Act of 1956, to meet civilian and military defence requirements by 1969. It was the greatest road-building program ever undertaken by any nation in the world, and would encourage American families to travel even more. By 1955, it had already been documented that automobiles visiting the national parks in America had increased by 112 percent 1946.

A 1956 study reported that the current automobiles being built lasted twice as long, despite the fact that recorded mileage was on the average 4½ times greater than it was 30 years ago.

A total of 2,005,432 four-door sedans were built in America in 1956, which, after the buyer frenzy of 1955, turned out to be a good, average year. The sudden slower pace, however, resulted in initial overproduction and sales were discounted to get rid of stock. While the "Big Three" could afford this market adjustment, the two smaller independents suffered. Packard's hopes had been high for a better 1956, but just as its new line was about to make its debut on 1 September, a strike shut the factory down for ten days. This delayed

There were comparatively few styling changes for 1956, but the new grille and two-tone paint treatment made this Chevrolet immediately recognisable from every angle. The wider, V-shaped grille afforded the Chevy a lower, road-hugging look. The four engine choices consisted of a 140hp ohv six; a 162hp V8 with a manual shift; a 170hp V8 with the Powerglide automatic; and a Super Turbo-Fire 205hp V8. The base model Two-Ten is pictured.

the introduction for nearly two months, while rear-axle problems caused a recall of 5,000 Packard models. The problem was supposedly fixed, but all the cars had to be recalled yet again. In 1956, Packard halted production in Detroit altogether. The company needed to sell 65,000 cars to break even, but production struggled to peak at just 28,325.

Studebaker sales, meanwhile, were down by 46,000 units, and over at American Motors, even Rambler sales were down almost 5,000 units, with Nash sales well below 20,000 and Hudson under 10,000. Overall market share for Studebaker-Packard and American Motors, the last two independents, thus fell from 4.5 percent to a meagre 3.2 percent.

Comparing sales figures for the newly merged companies over the previous ten years, the American Motors figure for 1946 was 193,769 cars versus the 1956 total of 104,895 cars delivered. Studebaker-Packard's total in 1946 was 119,668 cars against 93,387 in 1956. To put this in an even clearer perspective, Chevrolet alone built 397,109 cars in 1946 versus the 1,621,018 in 1956. Thus did the "Big Three" continue to grow bigger, even when competing head-on with each other for market share. Over the next three years, GM, Ford and Chrysler would learn the hard way that not every innovation, design and model they built would be a success.

Above: The majority of styling changes on the '56 Chevrolets were seen in the interior. Directional turn signals were standard on the entire 19-model lineup.

Right: The 1956 Chrysler Windsor V8 four-door sedan, with its three-speed column-mounted shift, sold well, achieving over 60,000 units. Some options offered included power windows, steering and brakes, front seat air conditioning and even a Highway Hi-Fi record player.

The 126in-wheelbase Chrysler Windsor underwent a facelift, losing its twin grilles in favor of three horizontal chrome bars with chrome surround, whereas its rear fins grew in height. The Windsor was the entry level into a line of high-priced four-door family sedans that combined considerable luxury with V8 performance. Standard features included a 12-volt battery, Oriflow shock absorbers, safety door latches, an independent parking brake, safety rim wheels and improved brakes.

The higher-priced New Yorker model shared a family resemblance, with subtle styling refinements to set it apart. The front headlamp bezels were more stylized, the grille was more intricate and jewel-like, and the bumper was more integrated into the overall design. The St. Regis version was distinctive by its three-toning.

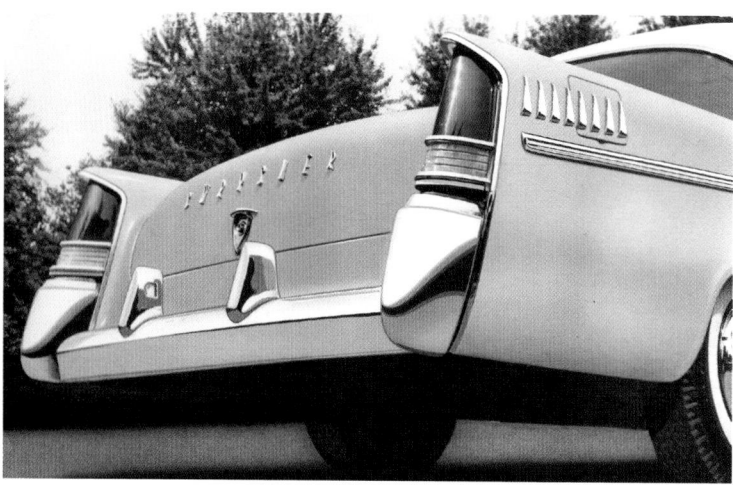

The New Yorker was also distinctive at the rear through its bold, fashionable taillight and bumper treatment. An added splash of chrome came in the form of faux rear fender vents.

Above: The New Yorker was Chrysler's luxury-market car, sharing its body with Chrysler's high-performance model, the more recent 300. Available only as a two-door hardtop, the 300B (the consecutive suffix letter marking its second year of production, in this case 1956) was continuing to make its mark in stock car racing. The New Yorker had the same Hemi 354ci V8 engine, but rated at 280hp rather than its counterpart's whopping 340hp. Still, today an owner of a New Yorker four-door sedan could easily turn it into a family express car.

Right: Mopar, derived from "Motor Parts," was Chrysler's factory parts supplier, established in 1937 at the request of Walter P. Chrysler for a brand name that would showcase the antifreeze used in the Chrysler family of cars. More Mopar products soon appeared on the market and in 1953, the division expanded both its plants and available parts and product range. Although the Mopar brand quickly began to stand for more than just antifreeze, it didn't become a household name until the muscle-car era of the 1960s.

Classic American Sedans of the 1950s: The Four-Doors

The 1956 Ford Fairlane outranked the Customline and Mainline models in the US. Sold in both a Six and Eight Series, both sported more chrome mouldings and stainless trim, while the V8's tailpipes passed through the rear bumper. It was cool-looking, but not highly practical. Power choices for the 115.5in-wheelbase, 198.5-inch long Fairlane included the 137hp 223ci six, the 173hp 272ci V8 or 200hp 292ci V8. Over 277,000 four-door sedans were built.

As a family four-door sedan, the big Fords were a great choice and went above and beyond what you'd expect. For 1956, the Fairlane and its siblings all came with a redesigned interior with optional padded dash and padded sun visors. The steering wheel had a new "deep dish" recessed hub, which supposedly reduced chest injuries in an accident. Also optional for the first time on a Ford were seatbelts, though buyers were not overly impressed and, ten years later, when the government and insurance companies complained about motoring deaths, the industry declared "Safety doesn't sell!", which led to mandatory regulations.

The all-new four-door Lincoln Capri looked big and was big at 223in long. It also had the distinction of bearing the largest windshield in the industry. At $4,212 it was pricey too, with 4,436 sold. Lincoln added to the marque's prestige with the introduction of the separate Continental MKII brand, which at a price of retailing at $10,000 was the most expensive car in America. The once high-end Capri was now a step below the similar Premiere model.

What price luxury? The scripted name badges and hood ornament on the nearly identical Premiere were adorned in gold at a cost of $4,601, distinguishing it from the lower-cost Capri. The total number of four-door sedans sold was 19,465, rivalling sales of the sportier two-door.

Compared to the Chevrolet, the 1956 Pontiac was a bit of a styling disaster. While Chevrolet's prestige soared, the Pontiac, for all its sound engineering, had an image of an old Auntie's car. Management realized this, and in 1956 appointed a young fellow by the name of "Bunkie" Knudsen was named general manager. He would immediately start to turn the division around, but, for the moment, the heavy bumper, unattractive "sucker" grille, chrome-laden hood and headlights could at least be redeemed by being in different colors, and particularly so when in two-tone.

The Pontiac V8 was a 316.6ci engine rated at 192, 205, 216, and 227hp. When fitted with the 227hp unit, the Star Chief four-door sedan was capable of 0–60mph in just 11.4 seconds and of achieving the quarter-mile in a time of 18.1 seconds. Performance was going to be a big part of the Pontiac rebirth, and to that end the 317ci engine was revamped again and became known as the 285hp "NASCAR" engine. Performance helped sell Pontiacs in 1956 to the tune of 405,730 units, putting the division sixth in overall sales in America.

New sheet metal saw the 190hp Studebaker President V8 sporting raised fenders, hood and trunk, which made it the largest car in the low-priced field. All Studebakers were in this category, with the Packard side of the company catering to higher-priced models. The squared-up hoods and trunks of the sedans also made them appear larger, while the President models were distinguished by unique side moulding, two-toning and additional chrome.

The 3,140lb Commander was powered by Studebaker's 170hp, 259.2ci V8. Commander sedans stripped of external trim were sold to police departments, but were powered by 185hp versions of the same engine. Sedan "Police Specials" were also sold with 289ci V8s. Starting in 1956, Studebakers came equipped with 12-volt electrical systems.

Rear fins were a fashionable styling cue on virtually all American car models by 1956, including four-door family sedans. Fin sizes varied only slightly at this point, but would soon grow in height and expanse, further mimicking aircraft tailfins and wings. In comparison, Studebaker's range was designed with subtle fins, such as those seen on this Commander.

This 101hp, six-cylinder 1956 Champion was assembled in California in late 1955. In total, Studebaker built approximately 17,000 of these stylish Champions. (Image courtesy of owner Nick Jonkman)

Chapter 8
1957 Detroit and Designers Losing Touch?

*P*opular Mechanics magazine of March 1957 asked its readers what they thought of the 1957 American car line-up. One reader remarked, "The rear end of the average 1957 car looks at you like a pig-eared donkey," while many complained about overall size and bulk. Others noted that the ubiquitous wrap-around windshields didn't add much in the way of improved visibility, but did make ingress and egress awkward. Another reader stated his opinion in no uncertain terms: "The way Detroit believes that style is all-important and engineering is secondary is nauseating. I, for one, am revolting against the trend."

In actuality, numerous readers of this publication had decided to buy a smaller British or European car for better quality, size and economy, which was an early sign that, over the following two decades, imported cars would make huge inroads into the American automotive market. In North America, Volkswagen was leading the import charge, followed by dozens of other German, British, French and Swedish automobiles. Even some eastern European marques were finding buyers.

Though operating on a much smaller scale than the USA, Canada was seeing similar exponential manufacturing and sales expansion over a 30-year period. In 1927, automakers sold 146,421 cars and 340,616 in 1957. Out of the latter total, 186,559 were four-door sedans, well ahead of the 56,147 of the second most popular body style, the two-door sedan/coupe. American Motors' Canadian sales were also struggling by 1957, with just 1,792 cars sold, well behind the 5,468 units shifted by Studebaker-Packard.

To put the remaining independent automakers' position in perspective, third-place Chrysler Corporation built 69,421 models, while Ford produced

Although looking very stylish, this 1957 Nash brochure cover conveyed a mixed message. The elegantly dressed couple doesn't appear to be heading out on a road trip to take advantage of the sleeping-in-car design the company was well known for by this time. The car's front-end styling was unique with its round grille and hood ornament plus stacked dual headlamps, a craze that would sweep the industry in 1958, though more often these were horizontally placed. A round grille would also appear on Ford's new Edsel, but buyers did not embrace it on the Nash and would not on the Edsel either.

109,889. Interestingly, Canadians weren't impressed with the new Edsel either, buying only 3,537 to put into their garage; more than twice as many Monarchs were sold. The most popular cars in Canada in 1957 were built by GM, which achieved a total output of 153,417 that year.

An auspicious event that brought extra hoopla and sales in 1957 was the 60th anniversary of Oldsmobile and Pontiac (originally founded as Oakland), while in the other camps, Plymouth built its ten millionth car and Ford produced its three millionth Mercury. However, a significant departure from practice this year resulted from the annual meeting of the board of directors of the Automobile Manufacturers Association, whereby a resolution was adopted to exclude speed and racing from automotive advertising and publicity. Ironically, the influence of factory teams and sponsorship in stock-car racing, drag racing and rallying increased, with the horsepower race continuing to heat up.

Owning a Cadillac one day was the dream of many in the 1950s. Big, powerful, and luxurious with lots of glitzy style, a Cadillac was seen as the icon of financial success in the eyes of many North Americans. While Lincolns and Imperials were alternatives, it was Cadillac that set the benchmark. You wouldn't find them at motels and campgrounds, or even at those new Howard Johnsons or Holiday Inns; a Cadillac-owning family was more likely to enjoy an exclusive resort or a Waldorf Astoria-like hotel. Today, fifties Cadillac sedans are still more expensive to buy or restore than a Ford or Plymouth, but the dream of acquiring one is in closer reach for today's enthusiasts.

In the eyes of the general public and die-hard Chevrolet enthusiasts, the lower and longer 1957 Chevrolet Bel Air is the pinnacle of 1950s Chevy style and desirability. Chevrolet built 254,331 four-door Bel Airs, 52,266 Series 150s and 260,401 Series 210 sedans. While the convertibles, hardtops and Nomads are big-ticket items, the 115in-wheelbase four-door family sedans all contain the same ingredients and similar icing. This unrestored but solid example has gobs of potential.

1957 was the only year in which Chevrolets were styled with a pronounced vertical fin. In 1958, it would be curtailed, only to reappear in its bat-wing guise in 1959 and 1960. Still, of the tri-Chevs, the '57 is the most sought after, especially if powered by the new fuel-injected 283hp, 283ci V8 also offered on the sporty Corvette as well as the new big Chevy. It was the first American block ever to develop 1hp for every cubic inch of displacement.

As well as a choice of eight engines, another option in 1957 was the first production fuel-injection system on an American car. Otherwise, the standard V8 was the 162hp, 265ci V8. Despite all the acclaim then and today, in 1957 Chevrolet finished behind Ford in model-year sales for the first time since 1935, and in the calendar year, only outsold Ford by a mere 131 cars.

Chrysler products were endowed with the biggest fins in the industry in 1957. In Canada, Dodge had two lines; one like the US models and the other based on Plymouth's line. The Canadian Dodge line, with its Plymouth body, had its own unique Dodge-like grille available as the Crusader, Regent and Mayfair. Otherwise, these Dodge models were identical to the Canadian Plymouth Plaza, Savoy and Belvedere. Power came in the form of the 132hp 250.6ci six, which was optional in the Mayfair, while the other models were fitted with the 302.5ci V8.

While the Canadian Dodge is rarer, the cult collectible 122in-wheelbase Dodge Royal models were and still are prized. The lesser Coronet shared the same styling, but lacked the pizzazz. The base Royal V8 (pictured) was a fine car, but the fully trimmed and equipped Custom Royal is the crème de la crème, especially when powered by the 340hp, 354ci Hemi V8. Then again, this powerhouse V8 was available in all models, making it one fast four-door family sedan.

1957 marked the end of the line for the once proud Hudson nameplate. Apart from new colors, changes in side trim, added die-cast fins, a flatter roof and smaller 14in wheels, which lowered the Hudson by two inches, it was virtually identical in appearance to the '56 model. Unique to Nash and Hudson was the pull-on-the-gear-shift-lever starting, which had been improved. Like the Nash, no six-cylinder engine was offered for the Hudson. Only 1,345 Hudsons were sold in the calendar year of 1957.

The Canadian Meteor used the new Ford body on its 116in-wheelbase Niagara and Deluxe Niagara 300 models. The Meteor Rideau and Rideau 500 (pictured) models sat on a 118in wheelbase. Standard power in the Rideau 500 was the 212hp, 292ci V8 with the new 245hp, 312ci V8 being optional.

Above: In March 1957, *Popular Mechanics* printed an "Owners Report" on the 1957 Ford. Owners from 38 states reported the Ford's styling and handling as its best features, while its worst were build quality and poor fuel economy. Yet, a total of 24 percent traded in a different make for the Ford and only 12 percent said they wouldn't buy another. Ford owners particularly liked the long and low look.

Left: Inside, the ash tray was a big complaint and the fact that the high transmission tunnel required the centre passenger to ride with their knees doubled up. The windshield A-pillar dogleg also proved troublesome for some.

1957: Detroit and Designers Losing Touch?

CUSTOM FOUR-DOOR SEDAN V-8 OR "6" Fits your family to a "T." Brilliantly styled family sedan—six passengers big, with plenty of luggage space for vacation travel. And it's loaded with luxury comforts you would never expect to find in any but the highest-priced cars.

SUPER FOUR-DOOR SEDAN V-8 OR "6" Try to match this beauty for practical family use. Its wide, wide seats and generous leg-room enable six six-footers to ride all day in solid comfort. Available in many new solid colors and two-tone combinations.

In 1957, the rear-mounted continental tire was still offered and still popular as many felt it provided a classy look. Aftermarket continental kits were, and still are, available and popular with hobbyists. While American Motors' styling was not unattractive, it did look like a traditional, conservative mom and pop's car when compared to a '57 Chevy.

The Nash Ambassador Custom four-door sedan was a large, comfortable, 121.3in-wheelbase family car. *Motor Trend* of July 1957 criticized the styling, brake pedal placement and wallowing, but concluded that the, "...superior body construction, generous interior proportions, reliable engine and plenitude of minor convenience make the Nash a car well worth its price."

1957 NASH AMBASSADOR SUPER FOUR-DOOR SEDAN —Here's the biggest room, the biggest value per dollar on the automobile market today. Compare it with the costliest cars for size and luxurious comfort.

The Nash and Hudson models in '57 were virtual twins. The Nash was also lowered by two inches through having its roof flattened and switching to 14in wheels. Both the Nash and Hudson were offered on a 122¼in wheelbase and were powered by the same 190hp, 255ci V8. Optional was a higher compression 255hp V8, while the six-cylinder models were discontinued. These last Hudson and Nash models were often unceremoniously called Hashes.

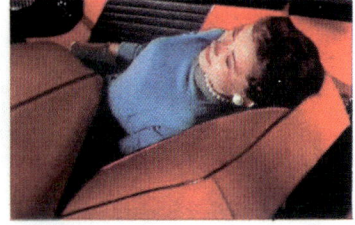
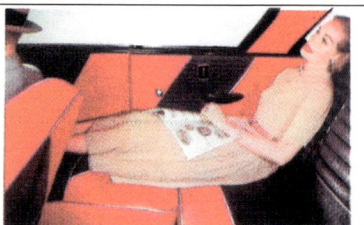

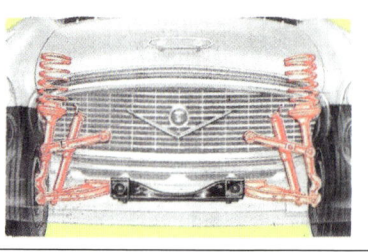

AIRLINER RECLINING SEATS, adjust to five comfortable positions to let you relax or doze the miles away while someone else drives.

EVEN A CHAISE LONGUE! Here is an instant "nap couch" for youngsters or a relaxing day-bed for grown-ups.

SLEEP WHERE YOU LIKE —with Nash Twin Travel Beds—No need to worry about reservations—no bother with tents or cots.

THREE TIMES SMOOTHER! Deep Coil Springs (on all four wheels) have three times more bump-absorbing capacity than old-style short, stiff springs.

With the end of the Nash line came the end of the convenient family sleeping car. While the Nash suspension allowed for a smooth, quiet and comfortable ride, the press reported roll and excessive leaning in fast turns.

The Hudson and Nash were excellent, well-built cars for family comfort and provided ample luggage space. In appearance, the Hudson changed little from 1956, while the Nash received a facelift in 1957.

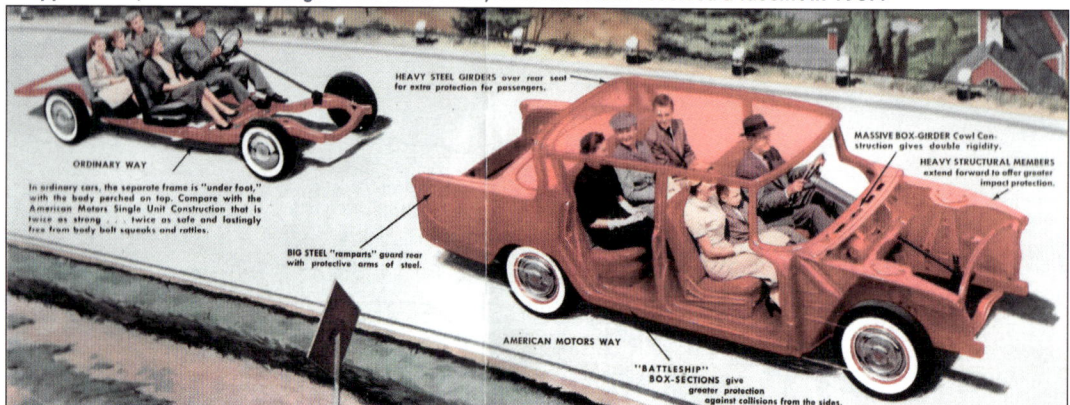

The American Motors Rambler had been well received by buyers and became the firm's volume-selling economy and compact car in 1957. V8 performance was also offered; in December 1956, *Motor Trend* tested a four-door Custom sedan fitted with a 190hp V8 and took it to 60mph in a credible 13.4 seconds, additionally recording 13.4mpg at 60mph. The magazine also praised the Rambler's good economy and decent performance, describing it as having "...better-than-average roadability."

The front end treatment on the all-new '57 Plymouth was even more distinctive than the rear. Its toothy grille was not well received by the press but, styling aside, the Plymouth was praised for its soft ride, better steering and handling on corners. *Motor Trend* of December 1956 concluded "...it definitely does not corner like a sports car. But it corners well, especially at higher speeds with no strain on unanchored passengers (even those in the backseat)."

The wheelbase of the Plymouth was 118in with an overall length of 205in. The six-cylinder L-head engine was rated at 132bhp. A comparison test found that the Plymouth achieved better fuel economy, but was less powerful than the Ford or Chevrolet. Prices ranged from $1,899 to $2,777.

Chapter 9
1958
The Year of Successes and Failures

As an additional $1.8m was allocated to speed up the interstate highway system, a total of four automotive milestones made the big news in 1958. The Ford Motor Company built its 50 millionth vehicle, Chrysler Corporation assembled its 25 millionth, General Motors Corporation had its 50th birthday and Ford celebrated the 50th anniversary of the Model T.

Studebaker-Packard announced the dropping of the Packard name, while Chrysler purchased 25 percent of Simca of France. Checker, better known for its taxis, announced plans to introduce the Superba passenger model, and Mercury introduced its little-remembered Medallion economy model.

Though Americans were beginning to buy smaller foreign cars in quantities that made Detroit take notice, American automobiles were getting larger; the 1958 Chevrolet, for example was 9in longer and 4in wider than the '56 model. The longest car of all in this model year was the new Lincoln, measuring 229in, four inches longer than the '57.

The "Big Three" manufacturers would begin to respond to the growing number of smaller imports by introducing "compact" cars such as the Valiant, Corvair and Falcon as the decade concluded. These

Like most auto plants in North America in 1958, Ford's Rouge plant expected high production and sales records, but that would not be the case. Nevertheless, Ford assembled around 800,000 full-size Ford cars that year.

cars would also compete head-on with the Studebaker Lark and the AMC Rambler. The 1958 Rambler Ambassador was actually shorter by nine inches compared to the Nash Ambassador.

Consumer Reports (*CU*) noted in its January 1958 edition that automakers and a lot of the press were emphasizing styling as a buying point rather than engineering. The magazine stated, "*CU* does not want its readers to forget that any car is a vehicle, and that outstanding vehicles have no obligation to be good looking, though they often are." A rather sober viewpoint.

And, as for the new Edsel, *CU* succinctly concluded, "In *CU*'s judgement, based on road tests, the car proved to be disappointing." Ford had made the Edsel a separate division to enhance its status, but the car itself was a sales flop and, even worse, became the butt of jokes nationwide. The press, conversely, gave the Edsel rave reviews, and despite first-day sales of 4,000 units, by the end of the month it was obvious that few wanted what Ford had described as "The Newest Thing on Wheels." Ford had figured on a production run of 200,000, but only 63,110 of all the 1958 Edsel models were sold, despite all the hype.

Overall, 1958 was a terrible year for the auto industry, due to the worst recession since the Great Depression. Sales were down by 31 percent over the previous model year, the hardest hit being Chrysler, whose production slumped 46 percent.

In a bad year for the industry, only American Motors' compact Rambler made gains in the market in 1958. In a full line of six- and 8-cylinder four-door sedans, the "American" was the base model, but was offered only as a two-door. The four-door Six Series 10 was offered in Deluxe, Super and Custom trim, and then came the mid-range Super model, which was purchased by nearly 30,000 buyers, around twice as many as the other two. *Consumer Reports* (May 1958) observed that the Rambler Six tended to pitch, and its ride and handling weren't the best, but it was nonetheless "...well-finished, compact, quiet, smooth and solid."

Classic American Sedans of the 1950s: The Four-Doors

AMBASSADOR CUSTOM 4-DOOR SEDAN

The well-dressed Ambassador Custom was priced at $2,732 compared to just $2,047 for the lowly Deluxe Six sedan. Optional equipment included the classy continental rear-mounted spare. The Rebel and upmarket Ambassador V8 sedans were not nearly as popular, selling fewer than 5,000 and 9,000 units, respectively.

Left: This Rambler Custom wears its original pink and white colors. Pink, yellow, turquoise green, blue, bright red and salmon colors were all the rage in the last half of the fifties. Much of the general appeal for late-1950s cars lies in the amount of chrome, pastel colors in two and three-toning and tail fins, and the Ramblers certainly followed that trend.

Below: The top-of-the-line four-door Ambassador rode on the same 108in wheelbase as the other Ramblers. The Ambassador was set to be introduced as a Nash and Hudson, but was dropped almost immediately, although a few may still exist.

The Ambassador Super 4-Door Sedan is unmatched for smooth-flowing style and scintillating performance—all at a very modest price. Here is the car for Canadian families on the go . . . the sleek beauty that is equally at home at the country club . . . the office . . . or on the open road. Compare it, feature for feature, with any car within hundreds of dollars of the price. We are confident you'll agree—"This is the car for me!"

Symmetry of design and conveniently-located controls within easy reach of the driver are features of the new decorator-styled Ambassador instrument panel.

Interior and exterior color schemes harmonize in the Ambassador Super. Seats—both front and rear—are extremely wide and comfortable. And the distinctive hardware and appointments blend to form a harmonious whole.

Right: In 1958, the press praised the all-new X-frame, the 209in-long, full-size Chevrolet Biscayne sedan's performance and handling, and its big, long, low look. Sales of the more affordable and practical Biscayne, were spurred by Chevrolet's sporty Impala and Corvette, an example of which is seen in the background of this beach-themed advert. Corvette production numbers were low in American terms, its exclusivity making it one of the most desirable sports cars in North America. Chevrolet was thus becoming GM's halo brand, as well as being its highest production division.

Below: The 117.5in Chevrolet Biscayne (formerly the Two Ten) was the entry-level model, but featured all the engineering, power and admired styling cues without the added frills. The rear end styling came with mixed reviews – some liked the absence of fins, while others rejected the sculptured look.

The Tri-Chevs have always overshadowed the 1958 models, regardless of their close connection with the soon-to-be-legendary Impala. The styling and popularity, compared to the previous three years and the bat-wing that followed, have made '58s more affordable for Chevy enthusiasts. In the *Consumer Reports* test of May 1958 comparing American six-cylinder cars, the Delray was fastest by over a second compared to the second fastest Ford, with a 0–60mph of 15.5 seconds. Overall, despite its fine performance, *CR* stated that the Chevy suffered from "unpleasant noise, and from a ride which is generally harsh, together with more than a trace of poor workmanship."

The flashy De Soto was subject to only a mild do-over in 1958 and recorded its worst year since 1938, the basic 350ci V8-powered Firesweep four-door sedan finding only 7,646 buyers. Other bad news was the closing of all the designated De Soto-only plants; a sad way to celebrate De Soto's 30th anniversary. Although some Hemi V8s were sold with fuel injection, Chrysler began phasing out the engine due to cost, in favor of its high-performance wedge.

For 1958, Ford featured dual headlamps on its facelifted models. In the six-cylinder comparison test by *Consumer Reports* it finished on top, but the reviewer damned it with faint praise; "The Ford Six, as it happened with other '58 Fords tested, succeeds by virtue of a high, well-balanced mediocrity. It has no outstanding, remarkable abilities..." Collectors today might disagree, particularly with all the modern upgrades possible, not to mention parts availability.

For those wanting a luxury alternative to Cadillac and Lincoln, the high-flying Imperial LeBaron offered Chrysler's most dramatic styling, power, comfort and exclusivity for business or family use. Retailing for $5,632, the LeBaron four-door sedan found just 501 buyers, though the lesser Imperial Crown at $5,598 attracted 1,240. The entry-level Imperial sedan at $4,945 sold best, with 1926 units shifted. Buyers of the 1958 Imperials really wanted additional options; 93.6 percent added power seats, 92.6 percent requested power windows, 86 percent ordered whitewall tires and another 33 percent wanted air conditioning.

The styling of the all-new Lincoln Capri was a blend of the old and the outrageously styled Continental Mk. III. Standard features included automatic transmission, power steering and power brakes, windshield washers and a padded dash. Its new Lincoln 430ci V8 engine boasted 375hp. However, as well as getting to grips with the brand new Wixom factory, the new unitized method of construction resulted in structural problems, and along with the Capri's radical styling, contributed to declining sales.

A step up again was the Lincoln Premiere, which differed further with its gold eight-pointed stars and badging, stainless-steel rocker-panel trim and slightly different front and rear bumpers. Inside, a host of rich leathers were offered. Air suspension was also available, but just 2 percent opted for it. At a cost of $5,565, only 1,660 were built, making it a very exclusive sedan. This was Lincoln's first unibody design and first body dip method for prime painting. In spite of this, these models were unfortunately prone to rust and few Capri or Premiere sedans survive today.

OLDSmobility

The new way to travel that takes you out of the ordinary into the Rocket Age!

...and engineered for excellence throughout!

Oldsmobile for 1958 is engineered to be both rugged and right! For its new Rocket Engine is writing this year's big economy news . . . with multiple engineering advances that boost efficient action to a brand-new high! Just try it and see how new camshaft design . . . new manifold design . . . 10-to-1 compression ratio . . . all combine to make the '58 Rocket the road's most talked about performer!

Even comfort's calibrated to the nth degree in Oldsmobile . . . with exclusive New-Matic Ride*! For here is *true* air suspension. Four air cushions of tough rubber-nylon give you a variable rate ride, smooth and level whatever the road or load! It's a "closed system", too, meaning dependable performance with minimum upkeep.

And wait'll you see the brilliantly engineered accessories . . . like Oldsmobile's all-transistor Trans-Portable Radio*. It's actually *two* radios in one. With its own speaker and 160-hour batteries, the Trans-Portable plays inside or outside the car.

Wherever you go, you go with extra value in an Olds . . . with such features as Safety Plate Glass all around! Clearly the '58 Olds is a car in a class by itself! But judge for yourself . . . as your own test driver . . . in a Rocket road test soon!

*Optional at extra cost.

OLDSMOBILE DIVISION OF GENERAL MOTORS CORPORATION

FEBRUARY 1958 **255**

Engineering and power were stressed by Oldsmobile in 1958, while styling was closer in resemblance to its Buick sibling rather than a Pontiac or Chevrolet. Restyled, its questionable appearance was obviously liked by many as the division claimed fourth in model sales with 294,374 delivered. Most popular of the Super 88s was the four-door sedan at 33,844 units. Well optioned in luxury touches, the price came in at $3,112. Restoring one of these fine, chrome-laden "Rockets" today would not be for the faint of heart.

Above: It was the end of the line for the 1958 Packard Town Sedan, and as an automaker, Packard itself. Despite this, the Studebaker-Packard Corporation name would live on into the sixties. Of the coupes, hardtops, station wagons and sedans, only 2,622 Studebakers wore the Packard name. The 1958 model year ran from January to July and just 1,200 sedans were built, so this is a rare car indeed, although, in reality, is it just a well-dressed Studebaker? Nonetheless unique, with the extended nose, bigger fins, better ride, added glitz and the proud Packard nameplate above all of it, these rare four-door sedans are real crowd pleasers at car shows today.

Right: Retailing at $2,378, Studebaker's Commander four-door sedan differed only slightly in trim from the lower-priced Champion. The biggest change comprised standard dual headlamps, which were optional on the Champion. (Courtesy of owner Stephen Porter)

Classic American Sedans of the 1950s: The Four-Doors

The Studebaker Commander's rear fins and tail lights were also changed and resembled those found on the sportier Hawks. This was the last year for the full-size Studebaker models, as the corporation would pin all its hopes and future on the new compact Lark.

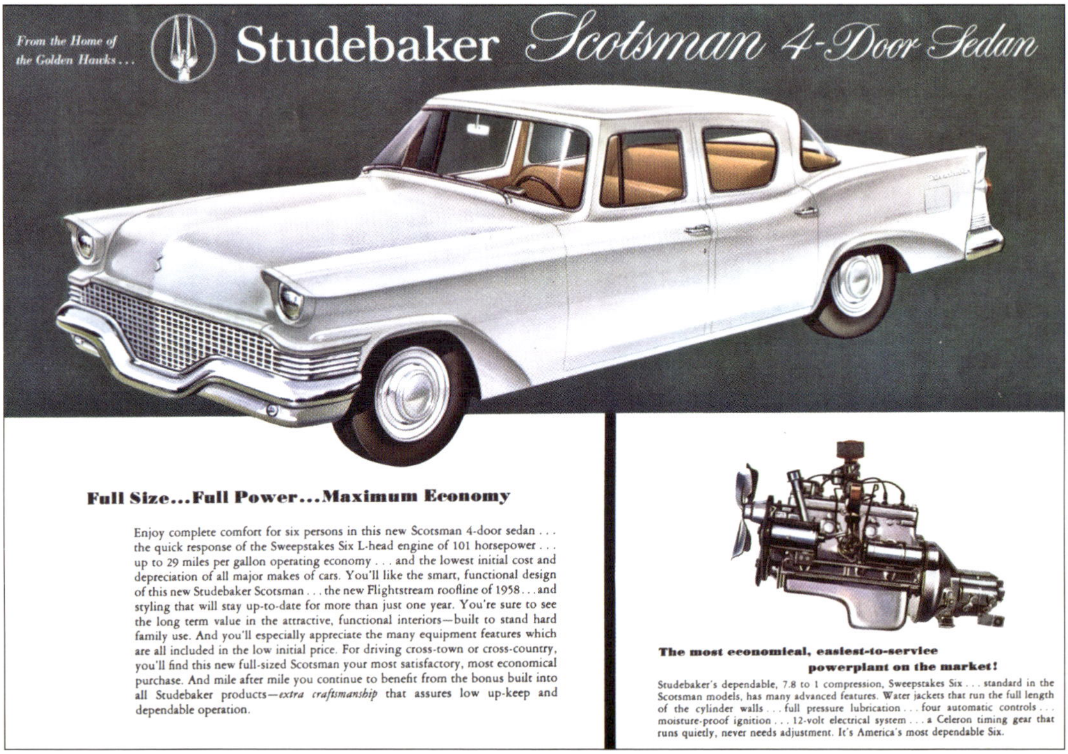

From the Home of the Golden Hawks... **Studebaker** *Scotsman 4-Door Sedan*

Full Size...Full Power...Maximum Economy

Enjoy complete comfort for six persons in this new Scotsman 4-door sedan... the quick response of the Sweepstakes Six L-head engine of 101 horsepower... up to 29 miles per gallon operating economy... and the lowest initial cost and depreciation of all major makes of cars. You'll like the smart, functional design of this new Studebaker Scotsman... the new Flightstream roofline of 1958... and styling that will stay up-to-date for more than just one year. You're sure to see the long term value in the attractive, functional interiors — built to stand hard family use. And you'll especially appreciate the many equipment features which are all included in the low initial price. For driving cross-town or cross-country, you'll find this new full-sized Scotsman your most satisfactory, most economical purchase. And mile after mile you continue to benefit from the bonus built into all Studebaker products — *extra craftsmanship* that assures low up-keep and dependable operation.

The most economical, easiest-to-service powerplant on the market!

Studebaker's dependable, 7.8 to 1 compression, Sweepstakes Six... standard in the Scotsman models, has many advanced features. Water jackets that run the full length of the cylinder walls... full pressure lubrication... four automatic controls... moisture-proof ignition... 12-volt electrical system... a Celeron timing gear that runs quietly, never needs adjustment. It's America's most dependable Six.

Studebaker's best-selling four-door Scotsman sedan was introduced late in the 1957 model year, the name being chosen due to the popular perception, socially unacceptable today, of Scottish thrift! Accordingly, its extremely basic nature was reflected in the cheap price of $1,799. Powered by a 101hp six, the only brightwork and chrome on the 1958 model were minor trim bits and the bumpers, although the bumpers were ultimately offered in paint to reduce costs even further. All the other trim was painted, including the hubcaps, and no two-toning was offered on the Scotsman models. Furthering the Scottish theme, the available colors included Glasgow Gray, Glen Green, Loch Blue, Midnight Black and Parchment White. A "Police Marshall" Scotsman came equipped with Studebaker's 289ci V8.

Chapter 10

1959
The Decade of Flamboyant Styling Ends and Power to the People Begins!

The decade ultimately dubbed the "Swinging Sixties" would prove to be a time of miracles, love, hate, war and heartbreak. Yet, during this socially turbulent epoch, the auto industry continued to grow and prosper. The horsepower race and 0-60mph times were about to become the most important factors in automobile purchases.

In 1959, all the issues that would characterize the 1960s were present, but had not yet reached their boiling point. In automotive terms, fifties styling, with its fins and chrome, had shot almost for the stratosphere on the 1959 Cadillac, Imperial and Plymouth. After this, fins would begin to shrink and were almost gone altogether by 1961. Making their simultaneous exit stage left after having reached their limit of popularity were two- and three-toning paint schemes in pastel colors.

Change was distinctly overdue; *Science & Mechanics* compared the latest four-door Ford, Chevrolet and Plymouth in April and concluded that, from a family point of view, all three had the same basic problems. Grandma, to start with, couldn't get into the back seat of any of them easily, and once seated, had no lower-back support, with her knees forced too high for comfort. Junior, for his part, was too big to seat himself, with his long legs over the driveshaft humps. Mom complained that in winter, those wrap-around windshield collected all the snow on the sides, turning them into huge blind spots. Mom also felt that she didn't need to haul two tons of car to the store just for a pound of butter.

In any case, buyers' tastes were changing. Hudson, Nash and Packard were gone, and the Edsel and De Soto were quickly going the way of the dodo. While hardtops and convertibles with lots of horsepower were proving to be an important factor for both image and prestige, most families were still buying four-door sedans and chose a six-cylinder for economy or a small V8. Still, the excitement surrounding the high-horsepower performance models was what drew customers into the showrooms.

Despite the fact that each division utilized many of the same basic engine blocks, in an early manifestation of what later became known as badge-engineering, the engineers within each division were given a great deal of latitude to develop their own methods of increasing the power. With fewer makes, buyers focused on their favorite manufacturer and had become a Ford, Chevy, Dodge, Studebaker, etc., family. Buyer loyalty was strong, but by the end of the 1960s, imports would have swayed many of the North American families away from buying American automobiles.

Above left: A taxi cab company dating back to 1923, Checker was to officially commence production of its first non-commercial model, the Superba, in June 1959. A labor strike and lack of dealers, however, pushed the "official launch" back to December 1959. Built on a 120in wheelbase, the Checker was powered by an aging 80hp, 226ci Continental in-line six-cylinder engine.

Above right: The Checker Superba was big, but looking at that picnicking family, not *that* big. Seating eight, perhaps ten if many were children, it was aimed more at the taxi and limousine market than seeking out volume sales to families. With its mid-fifties styling, the Checker had more in common with a London cab than a Chevrolet.

The renamed 1959 Buick line-up consisted of the luxury Electra, the mid-range Invicta and the low-priced LeSabre, and these all-new Buicks were proclaimed the most changed in the industry. Characterized by its particularly angular, bat-like wings, the Invicta pictured here otherwise shared the same basic body as the Chevrolet and its other siblings. The front end, meanwhile, featured unusual slanted headlamps and continuous chrome nearly surrounding the entire body. This styling provided the Invicta with its own unique character, especially as a four-door sedan. Production fell to nearly 35,000 cars, although much of that was due to a steel strike.

1959: The Decade of Flamboyant Styling Ends and Power to the People Begins!

Above: Chevrolet's dramatic rear-end bat-wing styling and horizontal teardrop taillights have always been a love/hate point with buyers. Apparently, when Ford designers first saw the new '59 Chevys, they perceived a significant threat to sales that year, yet the more restrained Ford models went on not only to win international awards, but outpace Chevrolet in calendar year sales. *Science & Mechanics* (April 1959) compared the four-door Fords, Chevrolets and Plymouths and felt that the biggest difference between the three cars was in their steering, with that of Plymouth considered the fastest and lightest for ease of control in traffic.

Right: The all-new 119in-wheelbase Chevys were lower, wider and roomier, yet headroom was increased by 1.5in. Extensive modifications were also made to the chassis, suspension and the engines, which offered a choice of the new detuned six as well as eight different V8s. As pictured in this advertisement, the two-tone Bel Air body was also wider than its predecessor, providing comfortable seating for six. Prices for 1959 ranged from $2,160 to $2,900.

Chevrolet interior stylists were not about to take a backseat to those bat-wing designers. From a practical point-of-view, the driver's seat and steering wheel were relocated, which aided visibility, especially when combined with a 74 percent increase in the rear glass area. From a styling aspect, the dashboard and steering wheel were given an equally dazzling design, with the result a combination of sport and the space age. Only Chrysler's push-button transmission and dashboard came close in pizzazz.

The Chrysler Saratoga's flamboyant lines were also distinctive in a year of thoroughly idiosyncratic styles. It was built on the long-wheelbase 126in chassis for an overall length of 220.6in, and its front end styling, with its expansive dollar grin, was unique, as were the side mouldings and the roof-colored insert that matched the side slash. The interiors on these Chryslers were opulent, with an optional swivel seat for ease of entry. Only V8 power was offered, in various versions of 383ci and 413ci engines. The "Golden Lion" badge was also the source of this year's advertising theme, and the press photo captures all the American glitz and glamor of the time.

1959: The Decade of Flamboyant Styling Ends and Power to the People Begins!

Edsel's slogan for 1959 after a disastrous first year was, "Makes History by Making Sense." It only made sense to 44,861 buyers. Somebody at Ford, perhaps the same executive who okayed the pushbutton transmission in the centre of the steering wheel, must have had a sense of humor, as the 1959 Edsel was publicly unveiled on Hallowe'en. Rather than a medium-priced model as before, the Edsel was now sold as a high end, low-priced car. This least expensive Ranger four-door sedan was built on a 120in wheelbase and power came from Ford's 200hp, 292ci V8. More power and glitz could be ordered on the Corsair. On 19 November 1959, Ford announced the Edsel would be dropped altogether after the current 1960 model, which had discarded most of the Edsel eccentricities to end up very much a Ford-like clone.

Late in 1958, the newly introduced '59 Ford Galaxie surpassed the Fairlane 500 to become the flagship model in the big Ford line-up. The Galaxie's C-pillar was more akin to the T-Bird design, creating what many enthusiasts feel was one of the best-looking Ford models ever. This $2,700 Galaxie V8 sedan was one of 183,108 built. In a year of ostentatious styling, the handsomely conservative Ford is even more understated.

The intricate multitude of juxtaposed chrome shapes on the 1959 Imperial's front end must have been a design nightmare, not to mention if it proved necessary to repair later. As the decade closed, styling and design was about to change dramatically, although luxury cars would try to resist this new trend towards simplicity.

In space-age dashboard design, Chrysler was the winner, hands down. Compared to some of the Corporation's designs, the Imperial's dash was more luxury than lunar. The push-button transmission was offered well into the 1960s and worked quite well. There was lots of chrome and brightwork on the fully loaded instrumentation, otherwise consisting of pushbuttons and warning lights. Barrel oil pressure, battery, fuel and temperature gauges, on the other hand, were fairly novel, not to mention the bar readout speedometer. Particularly noteworthy is that strange rear-view mirror location.

Above: Once again, the LeBaron (with 510 built), was top dog of the production-line Imperials, with all the equipment standard on the Imperial Custom and Crown models such as air conditioning, power everything and full carpeting. As well as from different trim and badging, the LeBaron also added richer fabrics, two-tone paint and whitewall tires. There was also a very exclusive Ghia of Italy custom-made "Crown Imperial," as opposed to the Imperial Crown series. Less than 4,000 of all the Imperial models were built in 1959.

Right: If you are seeking a classic "gaudy" fifties American land yacht, a 1959 Imperial would be a great choice. The styling from head to toe is so over-the-top, it's terrific!

The base model Pontiac in Canada was the Strato Chief and could be identified by its badging, side trim and lack of fender-mounted running lights. Pontiac's image continued to improve, through stock-car victories including the prestigious Daytona 500 and the Darlington 500. Pontiac also took the National Hot Rod Association's "Top Eliminator" title and was top dog at Pike's Peak. In addition, *Car Life* magazine chose the Pontiac Bonneville as a "Best Buy."

Classic American Sedans of the 1950s: The Four-Doors

Above left: In Canada, the Pontiac line consisted of a unique, less expensive Strato Chief, the Laurentian and the Parisienne. In the US market, these models were sold as the Catalina and Bonneville. They became known as the Wide Track Pontiacs, more for stance than handling, but the public loved them and so did the press, with *Motor Trend* awarding Pontiac its "Car of the Year" trophy. Like all Pontiacs in 1959, this Canadian Laurentian sported twin rear fins, and was longer and lower with an extensive line-up of V8s offered, including the NASCAR 345hp, 389ci Tri-Power.

Above right: While Pontiac shared its styling with its Chevrolet sibling, the two cars were quite different inside. Pontiac's interpretation of a stylish dashboard was more "form follows function," far different than that of the designers over at Chevrolet. There were also differences for Canadian and American consumers; in Canada the Pontiac line sat on the narrower Chevrolet track – a 1.7in difference – and were powered by the slightly modified Chevrolet engines that dated back to 1954. The non-original velour seat coverings and fuzzy dice date this pre-millennium restoration.

The 108.5in-wheelbase Lark was Studebaker's new compact car for 1959 and its last new car. Although it looked new, the Lark was powered by the old 90hp, L-head 169.6ci six or the 180hp 259ci V8. Inside, reclining seats were reintroduced, with the passenger side able to be reclined fully in a bed-like manner, much like the old Nash. A grand total of 48,459 four-door, family Lark sedans were built in 1959. A Studebaker from any year would be a good purchase but, like many American cars of this decade, rust is their biggest problem. Parts remain plentiful, however, thanks to the great support of the Studebaker Driver's Club. The Studebaker National Museum in South Bend, Indiana is one of the best automotive museums in North America.

Chapter 11

Restoring and Collecting American Four-Door Family Sedans of the 1950s

Hot-rodding and customizing American cars from the 1950s began surprisingly; back in the 1950s, keen owners often wanted to put their own stamp on their car – often the family car. Meanwhile, such luminaries as George Barris, Bill Cushenbery, the Alexander brothers and many notable others were chopping, Frenching and channelling colorful period coupes, hardtops and convertibles. When these professional metal artists needed another engine and transmission, trim, bumpers, fenders et al, they scavenged them from the flotilla of four-door sedans littering used-car lots, junkyards or farmers' fields.

As far as barn finds go, this 1952 Chevrolet looks pretty clean and solid, but still requires a thorough inspection. Although there is no old, dried oil stain underneath the engine and transmission, the fan needs turning to see if the engine is seized. Assume the brakes are seized and both the brake and fuel lines may be rusty. Inside, rodents might have nested in the seats, eaten the wiring and left a smell that will result in much of the interior needing to be replaced. Although this car has been stored inside, there will be possible rust issues from sitting on bare concrete. Nevertheless, the chrome and bodywork look basically unscathed, so, while minor repairs are to be expected, this is a great find.

By the 1970s, the old car hobby was in full swing, and fifties car restorations to original condition began in earnest. Once again, it was the convertibles, coupes and hardtops that were highly sought after, and once again the high-volume, four-door sedans provided the parts.

As noted in the Introduction, young families in the 1950s were drawn into showrooms by the swanky convertibles and hardtops, but ultimately settled for a more practical four-door family sedan. Those collectors of the 1970s and the succeeding decades were the children in tow back in the fifties, well-primed to fulfil their dreams.

While today, it is all very nice that there are literally thousands of beautifully restored fifties convertibles, hardtops, and coupes to see at car shows and in museums, in reality the basic four-door family sedan, once so prolific, is now a rare sight. As a result, it is the sedan that often draws the crowds today, because it was just like the one Dad or Grandad used to drive.

In the years leading up to the Millennium, car manufacturers and buyers moved away from coupes and convertibles to focus on sporty four-door sedans. Future collectors grew up viewing two-door models as inconvenient to load small items in the back, and for sitting in the cramped, barely accessible rear seat. And besides, those two doors were large and heavy.

The most attractive reasons for collecting a fifties four-door sedan today is that they came with all the glitz; they could be fitted with cooler, aftermarket wheels, be tricked-out mechanically or painted in a rainbow of colors, can still be purchased at a reasonable price compared to a convertible or hardtop model, and can easily haul the kids, dogs and all kinds of other stuff. Despite decades of attrition, a multitude of vintage fifties four-door sedans remains out there, as fixable barn finds, survivors, restored or refurbished examples.

Whereas a Packard Caribbean is the ultimate Packard of this vintage, it's in a very different value bracket. The Clipper was a separate model, bearing its own unique ship's steering-wheel badge rather than the Packard crest. A 1955 Packard Super Clipper family sedan is far from exotic, yet it is fairly rare. This stylish two-tone light green and white color combination was a real attention-getter, as can be seen here at an auction. A solid, clean example, it required little, if any, serious attention. Regular maintenance and unexpected repairs would not be difficult, given the ready availability of enthusiast and club support.

Although not an official motto of the United States Postal Service, the creed "Neither snow nor rain nor heat nor gloom of night stays these couriers from the swift completion of their appointed rounds" can be applied to many a car collector. Despite it being the dead of winter, this Ontario, Canada enthusiast is hauling home a very restorable 1950 Pontiac Silver Streak. Note the interior is filled with bits and pieces; always take everything, as small, seemingly inconsequential pieces add up in cost very quickly during a restoration. Excess parts can also be traded or sold to help finance your restoration.

Unless you have lots of cash, of course, the cost of restoration of any four-door family sedan will easily exceed its purchase price. (Better to restore that hardtop or convertible!) Such are the costs today that a rebuilt drivetrain or even a show quality paint job during restoration can result in a collector-car hole you will never dig yourself out of! As is the case with most things, you buy the best four-door sedan you can afford or what you personally can handle in the way of repairs.

Buying a four-door sedan to undergo a restoration from the ground up is costly, yet when it comes to restoring old cars, rational thinking is frequently set aside. Childhood memories are often the motivating factor, and while spending four or five times the market value for a four-door sedan seems like folly, there are worse ways to spend your hard-earned money. Our dreams come in all forms, and the fulfilment of a dream lasts a lifetime.

While clubs exist for every American marque, and the internet is a great marketplace for the restoration pastime, it is still easier to restore some vehicles than others. Chevrolet, Pontiac, Oldsmobile, Buick, Ford, Plymouth, Dodge and Studebaker models have excellent club support and a vast network of suppliers when compared to Lincoln, Edsel, Cadillac, Nash, Hudson, Packard, Frazer-Nash, Chrysler, DeSoto, Imperia, and Rambler. These latter makes are still worth collecting, but greater patience and hunting for parts may be required.

With that said, the year of manufacture is also important. While mechanicals are generally easy when it comes to fifties American cars, it is the trim, glass, badges/script, door handles – the little stuff – that can be difficult to find, even in the more notable marques. For example, finding bits and pieces for a 1950 to 1954 Chevrolet is far more difficult than any of the 1955-57 Tri-Chevs.

If originality is not your first and foremost concern in your 1950s four-door family sedan, then any make or model is a great choice. Certainly, the current trend is away from originality in collector cars and

Back in the late 1960s and early 1970s, purist restorers despised hot rodders and customizers for destroying collectible cars. Half a century later, that feeling has evaporated for the most part, as there are plenty of restored cars. The former purists are currently adding disc brakes, a dual master cylinder, electronic ignition, radial tires, a modern sound system, seatbelts, and updated automatic transmission. Some go even further, as seen on this 1955 Chevrolet with its larger mag-style wheels, dual antennas, chrome lake pipe exhaust and 350ci V8 engine transplant. Also common these days is removing the spare tire in order to haul a cooler, folding chairs and a complete tool box.

instead making them easier to maintain, better handling, comfortable, and in a word, more practical. And isn't that what the 1950s four-door family sedans were all about in the first place?

Note: Most of the American cars originally exported to Great Britain and the Commonwealth were built in Canada. Throughout the 1950s, Canadian specifications and the makes and models offered were often different from those built in the United States. The Vehicle Identification Number, or VIN, states the country of origin. Certain models differed in only minor ways, such as in trim, grilles, taillights and badging, but in a number of cases the bodywork was unique. Mechanically, some differed in engine specifications or were fitted with different engines altogether.

Restoring a Canadian-built family sedan may not be as easy as an American-built model, but parts are readily available and club support is strong. The resulting restored or refurbished four-door sedan would thus always be rarer and more unique than its American counterpart, but not necessarily more valuable.

Back in the 1950s, a four-door sedan was the perfect conveyance in which to transport your growing family. Today, it still is, as seen in this photograph of a modern-day family with their 1954 Studebaker Champion.

Other books you might like:

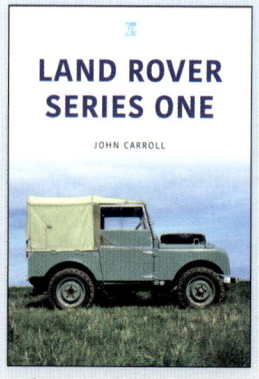
Classic Vehicles Series, Vol. 1

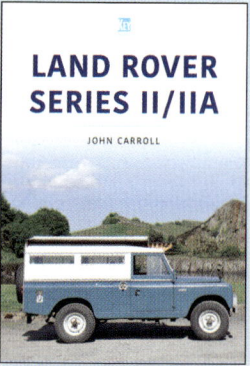
Classic Vehicles Series, Vol. 2

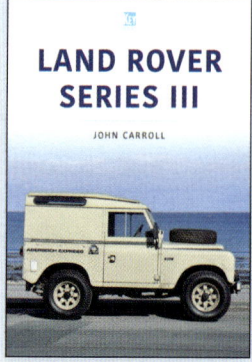
Classic Vehicles Series, Vol. 3

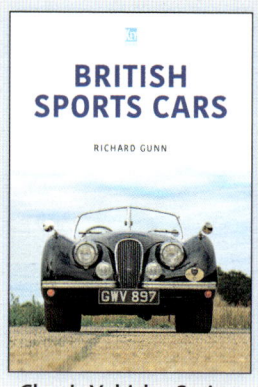
Classic Vehicles Series, Vol. 5

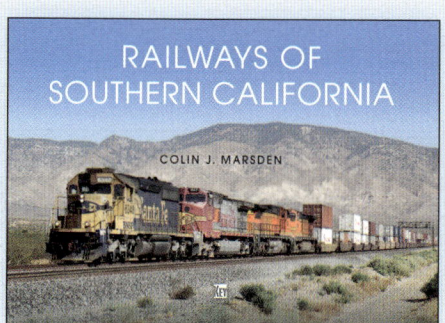

Classic Vehicles Series, Vol. 4

For our full range of titles please visit:
shop.keypublishing.com/books

VIP Book Club

Sign up today and receive
TWO FREE E-BOOKS

Be the first to find out about our forthcoming book releases and receive exclusive offers.

Register now at **keypublishing.com/vip-book-club**

Our VIP Book Club is a 100% spam-free zone, and we will never share your email with anyone else. You can read our full privacy policy at: privacy.keypublishing.com